THE
JERRIE MOCK
STORY

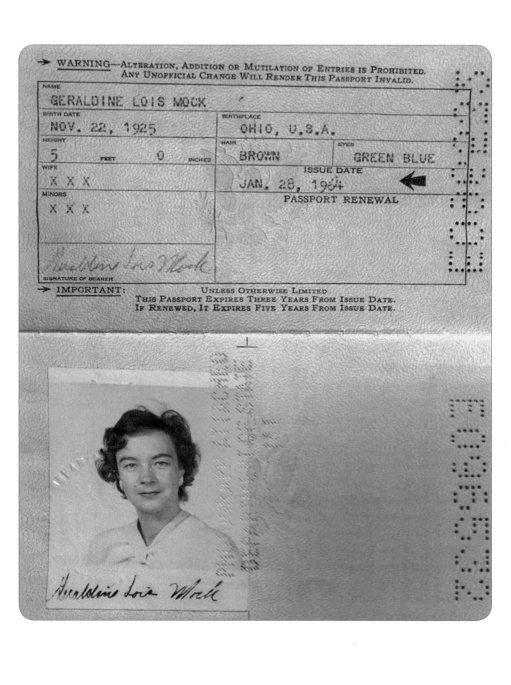

The First Woman to Fly Solo
around the World

THE
JERRIE MOCK
STORY

Nancy Roe Pimm

BIOGRAPHIES FOR YOUNG READERS

Ohio University Press
Athens

Ohio University Press, Athens, Ohio 45701
ohioswallow.com
© 2016 by Ohio University Press

To obtain permission to quote, reprint, or otherwise reproduce or distribute
material from Ohio University Press publications, please contact our rights and
permissions department at (740) 593-1154 or (740) 593-4536 (fax).

Printed in the United States of America
Ohio University Press books are printed on acid-free paper ⬡™

26 25 24 23 22 21 20 19 18 17 16   5 4 3 2 1

Frontispiece: In preparation for her flight around the world, Jerrie Mock
obtained her passport on January 28, 1964. *Susan Reid collection*

Library of Congress Cataloging-in-Publication Data

Names: Pimm, Nancy Roe, author.
Title: The Jerrie Mock story : the first woman to fly solo around the world /
  Nancy Roe Pimm.
Description: Athens, Ohio : Ohio University Press, 2016. | Series:
  Biographies for young readers | Includes bibliographical references and
  index.
Identifiers: LCCN 2015040787| ISBN 9780821422151 (hardback) | ISBN
  9780821422168 (pb) | ISBN 9780821445587 (pdf)
Subjects: LCSH: Mock, Jerrie, 1925–2014—Juvenile literature. | Women air
  pilots—United States—Biography—Juvenile literature. | Flights around
  the world—Juvenile literature. | BISAC: JUVENILE FICTION / Biographical /
  United States. | TRANSPORTATION / Aviation / History.
Classification: LCC TL721.M58 P56 2016 | DDC 629.13092—dc23
LC record available at http://lccn:loc.gov/2015040787

"Something hidden. Go and find it. Go and look behind the Ranges—
Something lost behind the Ranges. Lost and waiting for you. Go!"

—*from "The Explorer" by Rudyard Kipling, 1898*

Contents

BLUE SKIES ALWAYS

Author's Note

ONE EVENING while watching the local news, a story caught my attention. The news story celebrated the fiftieth anniversary of the first woman to fly solo around the world. Jerrie Mock had flown in her eleven-year-old plane from Port Columbus and landed twenty-nine days later at her hometown airport in Columbus, Ohio. The "flying housewife" had a compass, a map, and a system of dots and dashes to circumnavigate the globe. The longest leg of her flight took over seventeen hours, and at one point she had to stay awake for thirty hours. A war was going on. She flew over shark-infested waters. She landed in and took off from foreign countries with many different cultures and beliefs. *Incredible, amazing,* and *brave* were words that popped into my mind.

I always thought Amelia Earhart was the first woman to fly around the world. And as I started asking around, I found most folks think so. Not many had heard of Jerrie Mock. In 1964, the year Jerrie made history, so many stories were competing for the headlines: The Civil Rights Act had just passed. The Beatles came to America and appeared on the *Ed Sullivan Show.* The United States had just entered the war in Vietnam. The US and the USSR were in the middle of the space race.

When Jerrie Mock arrived home, she received a hero's welcome, and her story appeared on the front page of the local newspapers. She received numerous awards and recognition from high officials, even President Johnson! So why and how had Jerrie Mock been forgotten? Why didn't she have a prominent place in the history books? Why hadn't anyone ever heard of her?

I couldn't get Jerrie Mock's story out of my head, so I picked up the phone and gave her a call. "Airplanes were made to be flown," she said matter-of-factly. "You just got to use common sense, point it in the right direction, and be sure you have plenty of gasoline. The hardest part was planning; the flying was easy." I told her she was brave and daring. She laughed. "I was just having a little fun in my plane," she said. I tried to convince her that it was much more than that. I told her I would be honored to write her biography for young readers. I loved *her* story, an inspirational tale about believing in childhood dreams. It's something I talk about when I give author visits in schools. What's life without dreams and what's better than making dreams come true?

While researching her story, I set out to find the airplane she had flown. I went to the Steven F. Udvar-Hazy Center, an air-and-space museum in Virginia. My husband, Ed, and I searched for quite some time before we spotted the small red-and-white plane high above our heads, tethered to the ceiling. I had hoped to have a look inside the plane in order to see all the custom-made gas tanks and other adjustments that had been made for the long-distance flight, but that simply wasn't possible.

When I visited Jerrie, she sat in her recliner with a stack of books piled high on the table. At age eighty-eight, she spoke of her lifelong love of reading. As a young girl, she had read Nancy Drew mysteries, and, to that day, she still loved a good suspenseful story. Clearly a genius and a mathematical whiz, she pointed to her head while speaking about flying in races, and how she had made calculations to get an advantage over the competition. Her eyes sparkled as she recalled stories from long ago with amazing detail and passion. When I clearly had no idea who had been an enemy of Christopher Columbus, she pointed her finger at me and said, "Read your history books!" Jerrie still had an interest in history and geography, and she kept up with the news and current events. She asked about popular books kids were reading today, and she told me she hoped the younger generation knew the importance of reading books and of having a dream. During our visit, she referred to her book, *Three-Eight Charlie,* and asked me to include passages from this book she had penned in 1970. Her gift of writing was as brilliant as her gift for flying.

Soon after completing her flight she was quoted as saying, "I hope . . . that somewhere here and there my just doing something that hadn't been done will encourage someone else who wants to do something very much and hadn't quite had the heart to try it." With these words, and her life story to back them up, Jerrie Mock reminds us that even ordinary people can do extraordinary things. So work hard, put your heart into it, and follow your dreams!

CIRCUMNAVIGATING THE GLOBE

FLIGHT ONE

MARCH 19, 1964

No one would ever have believed that Jerrie Mock had a big day ahead of her. The thirty-eight-year-old woman straightened the house, packed a suitcase, and ran some errands. According to the *Columbus Dispatch,* "The petite Bexley housewife and mother went matter-of-factly about her business on the day before, and, like any woman about to take a trip, she had an appointment at the beauty parlor."[1] The next day she would leave to fly around the world. In 1964, there were very few female pilots, and even fewer who dared to fly alone for such a long distance. As Jerrie Mock planned her flight, she discovered that, if she succeeded, she would be the first woman to circle the globe, solo.

When the big day arrived, she finished packing her cramped little airplane, a Cessna 180 she had lovingly nicknamed *Charlie.* Three of the four seats had been removed, replaced with aluminum gas tanks, converting the single-engine airplane into a long-distance marathon flier. She squeezed a typewriter onto the pile of maps, a variety of snacks, her

THE CUSTOM-MADE FUEL TANK DESIGNED BY DAVE BLANTON BEFORE INSTALLATION INTO *CHARLIE*

Courtesy of Phoenix Graphix

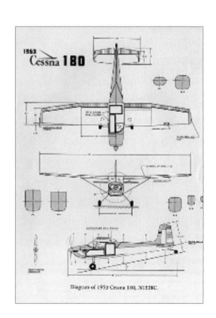

DIAGRAM OF 1953 CESSNA 180

suitcase, an oxygen tank, and a bulky life raft. Jerrie planned to write all about her journey and send her reports back to the local newspaper.

Jerrie's husband, Russ, and their two teenaged sons helped her fill the plane with emergency equipment and supplies. Their three-year-old daughter, Valerie, stayed at home with a neighbor because a big crowd was expected. Throngs of people swarmed around the tiny plane at the airport in Columbus, Ohio, in hopes of witnessing history. One reporter shoved the microphone at Jerrie and said, "Mrs. Mock, aren't you a little afraid? After all, no woman has ever done this."[2]

"Mrs. Mock, what do you think happened to Amelia Earhart? Do you think she's still alive somewhere?"[3]

Jerrie thought of her childhood hero, Amelia Earhart. Amelia had flown in races and set records. But there was one record she had wanted more than any other—to fly around the middle of the globe, the equator. On May 21, 1937, Amelia Earhart made her second attempt at the world record. Near the end of her trip, on July 2, 1937, she flew out of a small airport in Lae, Papua New Guinea. Earhart disappeared, never to be seen again. What had happened to the pilot is still a mystery to this day.

Jerrie needed to concentrate and keep things such as fear and disappearances out of her mind. She couldn't be bothered with all the questions. She had a plane to fly. Jerrie mentally went through her checklists. After all, she had a job ahead of her, and the reporters made her more nervous than the idea of flying over deserts and oceans. They persisted with their questions. Jerrie gave short answers as she stood by her plane in front of Lane Aviation, posing for one photo after another. She trembled with fright, suddenly realizing the enormity of what she was about to attempt. She smiled bravely, and kept her fear hidden. After all, people were counting on her.

The *Columbus Evening Dispatch,* her local newspaper, had promised its readers that she would "keep a careful record of her flight and her personal impressions."[4] A former Air Force pilot, Brigadier General Dick Lassiter, had met with Jerrie many times, helping her plot the best course to take around the globe, country by country. Major Art Weiner,

JERRIE POINTS OUT THE ROUTE SHE PLANS TO FLY, AS HER HUSBAND, RUSSELL, AND THREE CHILDREN, VALERIE, GARY, AND ROGER, LOOK ON

Reprinted with permission from the *Columbus Dispatch*

also with the United States Air Force, had spent countless hours preparing **navigation maps**, checking weather forecasts, and making flight plans. And, last but not least, her family supported Jerrie in her quest to follow her childhood dream.

Jerrie took comfort standing beside her eleven-year-old airplane while the photographers' flashbulbs popped. She wore a white shirt and a blue knit skirt under her blue coat, with high heels on her feet and pearls around her neck. *Charlie* sported a brand new red-and-white paint job with the words *Spirit of Columbus* emblazoned on its nose. She knew the single-engine Cessna was the best plane for such a flight.

JERRIE STUDIES WEATHER MAPS AND HER LOGBOOK AS SHE
PLANS HER ROUTE AROUND THE WORLD WITH HER JEPPESEN
FLIGHT COMPUTER IN HAND

Susan Reid collection

Charlie was tried and true, capable of flying around the world. One of
the reasons she had chosen a Cessna 180 was because she had been told
that with its high-set wings and powerful engine "a 180 could take off
with anything you could close the door on."[5] As Jerrie made plans to fly
around the world, she prayed. She had said, "I gradually felt certain that
God wanted me to make the trip and would see that I got home safely."[6]
And now her dream was becoming a reality. How could she turn back?

Russ came to Jerrie's side and steered her to their car. She needed
to go to the weather bureau and the flight service station in the nearby
Port Columbus terminal building to make a final check on the weather

LUCKY LINDY & LADY LINDY

JERRIE MOCK named her airplane *Spirit of Columbus* after
Charles Lindbergh's historic airplane, *Spirit of St. Louis*. Charles
Lindbergh, "Lucky Lindy," became a national hero when he flew
the *Spirit of St. Louis* nonstop from New York to Paris. His historic
flight in 1927 took over thirty-three hours. At times he felt like he
was asleep with his eyes open! In order to stay awake, he opened
the window and let the frigid air cool off his face. When asked why
his cat, Patsy, did not accompany him like she usually did, he said,
"It's too dangerous a journey to risk the cat's life."[7]

Amelia Earhart was called "Lady Lindy" by the press due to
her uncanny resemblance to Lindbergh. Amelia had once said,
"The most difficult thing is the decision to act; the rest is merely
tenacity." She flew over the Atlantic Ocean on June 3, 1928, accompanied by Bill Stultz and Lou "Slim" Gordon. Word spread, and
thousands came to greet the first woman to fly over the Atlantic.
When Amelia made her around-the-world attempt in 1937, she
was accompanied by **navigator** Fred Noonan. Amelia decided to
lighten her load when they were about to begin their long cross-
ocean flight to Howland Island. She boxed up and sent home
everything she didn't need for the flight, even her lucky elephant-
toe bracelet. "There must not be a spare ounce of weight left," she
said.[8] The only exception she made was for the five thousand
souvenir stamp covers kept in the nose cargo hold of her plane.
She planned to sell the autographed envelopes to help fund her
trip around the world. Sadly, Amelia Earhart and Fred Noonan disappeared, never to be seen again.

conditions and fill out an international flight plan. For official record purposes, there would be observers and timers at each stop to document every takeoff and landing for the NAA, the National Aeronautical Association, and the FAI, the Fédération Aéronautique Internationale. Howard Kenny, the head weather forecaster at Port Columbus, assured her that the weather looked good all the way to Bermuda. Once in the office of the flight service station, Jerrie was instructed to mark down her survival equipment. She completed the form, relieved that no one seemed to notice her trembling hand.

When all the necessary forms were filled out, Russ hurried Jerrie back to the Cessna, back to the crowds. Jerrie only wished to be alone in her plane, tucked away from the reporters, the microphones, and the endless questions. After all, she had a seven-hour flight ahead of her to the island of Bermuda, and she wanted to get going before her nerves got the best of her.

As soon as Russ opened the car door, the reporters hounded Jerrie with questions. She grew more annoyed with each one. As the cameras clicked, she hurried to the side of her plane and smiled bravely beside Governor James Rhodes of Ohio. Flashbulbs nearly blinded her as more photos were taken with Preston Wolfe, the publisher of the local newspaper. She posed with the wives of astronauts John Glenn and Scott Carpenter. An old friend nudged Jerrie and gave her a Bible to take along.

Jerrie's family gathered around. Her mom fretted. She had never understood Jerrie's adventuresome spirit, and she had always wished her daughter had an interest in something more down to earth, like knitting. Her sister Susan squeezed past a tall newsman and handed Jerrie a cup of hot coffee, while her sister Barb reminded her to collect stamps at every stop for her collection. Her dad told her to be cautious, and he promised to pray for her safe return. Jerrie's mother-in-law, Sophie, clasped a St. Christopher medal (the patron saint of safe travels) to Jerrie's coat and vowed to watch over her family.

Dave Blanton, who had developed the plane's fuel-tank system, gave her some last minute advice. He showed her how to put rags around

JERRIE POSES WITH HER MOTHER, BLANCHE WRIGHT FREDRITZ,
AND HER FATHER, TIMOTHY FREDRITZ

Reprinted with permission from the *Columbus Dispatch*

JERRIE'S HISTORIC FLIGHT MAKES FRONT-PAGE HEADLINES IN
THE *COLUMBUS EVENING DISPATCH*

Reprinted with permission from the *Columbus Dispatch*

the opening when filling up the airplane to keep the gas from leaking
into the **cockpit**. He stressed the need for plenty of rags, fresh rags at
every stop.

After all the preparations were complete, Jerrie removed her coat
to let Blanton and Russ place the cumbersome life jacket around her.
The well-wishers and reporters seemed to inch closer and closer. Jerrie
stood silently, but her insides shook. Blanton buckled the straps of the
life jacket while Russ walked around the airplane to make one final
inspection. Wearing a large straw hat, Jerrie climbed the high step to
the cockpit. She adjusted the two pillows behind her back and the one
underneath. Being only five feet tall, she needed the pillows to help her
see out the windshield.

When Jerrie was finally nestled in behind the controls in the peaceful cocoon of *Charlie,* Russ leaned into the cockpit. After giving her a
kiss, he reminded her to take plenty of notes so she would have lots of
good stories for the newspaper. Jerrie nodded and glanced over at her

JERRIE WITH DAUGHTER, VALERIE, AND HUSBAND, RUSS

Reprinted with permission from the *Columbus Dispatch*

two sons. They looked worried. Were they afraid that they might never see their mom again? She wished she could get out of her plane and give them one last hug.

Her head swirled from all the commotion, making it difficult to concentrate on her checklist. Jerrie reached for the master switch and the starter button on the left side of the panel. The engine rumbled as the propellers sliced through the air. Jerrie trembled with fear, wondering if she should call the whole thing off and rush back to her family. But she knew at this point going back wasn't really an option. So she went through one last checklist and taxied down to the long runway. Jerrie got on the radio and let the controller know she was ready for takeoff. His voice came across the radio giving her clearance to go.

At 9:31 a.m., Jerrie Mock pointed the nose of her aircraft toward the end of the runway at Port Columbus. Alone in her plane, she took a deep breath, and pushed in the **throttle**. *Charlie* barreled down the airstrip. Fire trucks and cameramen were lined up along both sides of the runway as they rolled past. The roar of the powerful engine thrilled Jerrie as the aircraft's wheels left the ground. The high-set wings of her plane lifted into the air and she trembled with excitement. Finally, after a lifetime of dreaming, she would see the world!

As the plane made its climb, heading east, Jerrie heard the tower controller say over the radio and the loudspeakers at the airport, "Well, I guess that's the last we'll hear from her."[9]

Jerrie Mock couldn't believe her ears. "I'll be back," she thought. "But I hope to never see him again."[10]

DID YOU KNOW?

Before Wiley Post flew out of Floyd Bennett Field in Brooklyn, New York, and became the first man to fly solo around the world, he worked as a professional pilot. Businessmen paid Wiley to fly them to their destinations. The experienced pilot earned worldwide fame with his record-breaking flight in 1933, but he already had earned worldwide fame as a race pilot competing in air derbies.

Jerrie Mock was not a professional pilot when she took off to fly around the world. She earned her private pilot's license in 1958, and six years later, with only about 750 hours of flying time behind her, she attempted her historic flight around the world. In order to fly around the world, she needed to get certification to fly her plane using instruments only. She became an instrument-rated pilot before she left the country, but she never had the chance to practice her new skill without an instructor sitting beside her before she left on her around-the-world flight.

Wiley Post was the first man and Jerrie Mock was the first woman to fly solo around the world. By coincidence, both of them also decided to elope when it came time to marry.

FLIGHT TWO

EARLY YEARS AND CHASING DREAMS

GERALDINE "JERRIE" Fredritz grew up in the small town of Newark, Ohio. Born November 22, 1925, to Timothy and Blanche Wright Fredritz, she was the oldest of three daughters. Jerrie was seven years old when her sister Barbara Ann was born, and she was fifteen when her youngest sister Susan completed the family. Every week her family attended Sunday services at the First United Methodist Church.

While Jerrie was still a young girl, her mom gave her strict orders never to cross the busy street in front of their home. But mostly boys lived on her side of the street. One day, after she arrived with a doll in her hand, the boys told her that if she wanted to play, she had better get rid of the baby doll. Jerrie quickly gave up baby dolls for hanging with the boys. She enjoyed their adventurous games, her favorite being cowboys and Indians. Camp Fire Girls meetings gave her a chance to be one of the girls.

Jerrie's interest in flying began at a very young age. When she was only seven years old, her mother and father took her to a small airfield

JERRIE'S FIRST CHILDHOOD HOME IN NEWARK, OHIO

Photograph by the author

near Newark, Ohio, during a local festival. The family of three climbed aboard a Ford Trimotor airplane. While in the air, Jerrie stared in amazement at the rows of rooftops, the cows in green pastures, and the tops of the trees. After the ride, she looked up at her mom and dad and said, "I love it! I'm going to be a pilot when I grow up." Her father patted her on the head and said, "Yes, dear."[1]

As a small child, Jerrie didn't know much about the world outside the little town of Newark. When her first grade teacher returned from a trip to Europe, she shared stories of the wonderful places she had been. "Most people in my town didn't travel anywhere. I had no idea what was out there." To quench her new thirst for adventure, Jerrie read lots of books. "I read books of all types," she said. "About half were fiction and half nonfiction."[2] Reading books let her travel in her mind, to places she could only dream about.

JERRIE AS A YOUNG GIRL
Susan Reid collection

In the fourth grade at Roosevelt Elementary School, Jerrie dove into her geography books, excited to learn about different cultures and exotic places. In her imagination, she rode across the Sahara Desert astride a two-humped camel in a long, loose dress with a veil draped over her head. "I wanted to see the world, all of it, the jungles, the deserts, and the

JERRIE AS A STUDENT
AT WOODROW WILSON
JUNIOR HIGH SCHOOL

Susan Reid collection

pyramids."[3] Whenever she heard that her hero Amelia Earhart was taking to the skies, she raced home to sit close beside the radio, keeping track of all the places Amelia visited in her plane. Jerrie wished one day to live such a fantasy life as Amelia's, flying from country to country.

Jerrie attended Woodrow Wilson Junior High School. At age eleven, she shared her dream of flying around the world with her girlfriends. They looked at her and laughed. One of Jerrie's friends dreamed of being a housewife, with lots of children, while the other one imagined herself as a movie star.

Jerrie graduated from Newark High School, but she never participated in sports. "At barely five foot tall, no one wanted me on their team. Besides, you have to consider the time. In the 1940s, girls didn't play many sports."[4] She played the trumpet and the French horn in the high school band, and she excelled at academics. In her senior year, she was the only girl in the advanced mathematics course. "World War II began, and advanced mathematics was offered to prepare the students to join the cause and fight the war," she said.[5]

In her junior year in high school, she took math with a class of seniors. One senior in particular caught her eye. He was the new boy in town, having just moved to Ohio from Connecticut. Russell Mock lived a block away, and they rode the bus together. He sat an aisle apart from Jerrie in math class. They argued about algebra, and he boasted about flying solo in a plane at age sixteen. At first they were just good friends, but soon they dated and went to dances. On weekends they made a mad dash to nearby Buckeye Lake Park, where they rode rides at the amusement park, swam at the swimming pool, and skated at the roller rink. When it came time for the senior prom, Jerrie arrived on the arm of Russell Mock.

After high school, in September of 1943, she attended the Ohio State University in Columbus, Ohio. Jerrie was the only woman studying aeronautical engineering; she also took an advanced chemistry class. Being the only female in a class full of male students raised some eyebrows. Some classmates poked fun at her and said the only reason she was in the class was to meet a husband. When she received the only 100 percent on a difficult chemistry test, she silenced their teasing.

In 1944, a career in aviation didn't seem realistic to Jerrie. Most girls her age were getting married and starting families. At the age of nineteen, Jerrie Fredritz dropped out of college to marry her high school sweetheart, Russell Mock. Since Jerrie didn't want all the fuss of a big wedding, she and Russ quietly exchanged vows in a courthouse, their ceremony conducted by the justice of the peace. Within two years they had sons, Roger and Gary. Valerie, their only daughter, came along twelve years later.

Jerrie found a way to satisfy her thirst for knowledge while caring for her babies. The Ohio State University had a radio program that taught Spanish, German, and French. Jerrie recorded the radio lessons and practiced speaking foreign languages while changing diapers and rocking babies.

While living in Bexley, Ohio, Jerrie and Russ enjoyed gourmet cooking and hosting three-course dinners by candlelight. After discussing which country to visit that evening, they set the table according to the traditions of the country and created exotic dishes from that part of the world. They welcomed many foreign exchange students into their house and learned their customs and traditions. Jerrie especially loved learning about the foods their visitors ate, and how they cooked their meals.

In the late 1950s and early 1960s, most women stayed at home with their children. Russ worked full-time as an advertising executive, and Jerrie worked part-time at many different jobs. Since the couple shared a passion for the opera, Jerrie talked about the Metropolitan Opera on the air for a local radio station on Saturday afternoons. She also hosted a local television show on Sunday afternoons called *Youth Has Its Say.*

JERRIE AFFECTIONATELY NAMED HER LUSCOMBE *TWEETY BIRD*

Courtesy of Phoenix Graphix

Every week, she chose four students from different schools in the Columbus area. The youths debated everything from global politics to a woman's place in the home.

Jerrie and Russ purchased their first airplane in 1952, and affectionately named the 1946 Luscombe *Tweety Bird*. In September of 1956, Jerrie took her first solo cross-country flight, a requirement for getting a private pilot's license. She flew her blue-and-white airplane to Kelley's Island on Lake Erie. After a successful landing, she sat on the runway, helpless. She needed to head back to Columbus to complete her solo flight, but *Tweety* had no starter and no electrical system. She had to spin the plane's propellers by hand and, being only five feet tall, it was impossible. Russ had always helped her to start the engine, and she assumed there would be someone on the island to assist her. Luckily, before the sun set, a pilot stopped by the airport, spun *Tweety*'s propeller, and sent her on her way.

One day, some friends invited Jerrie to join them on their Sunday morning routine of flying to an airport on the Indiana border for breakfast. Jerrie had a bad feeling and decided not to join the group of young men. During the flight, one of the planes came up behind the other and knocked its tail off. Both planes went down. No one survived. Shaken by the tragedy, Jerrie stopped flying briefly. When she resumed flying, Jerrie flew solo, renewing her permit year after year, not yet ready or willing to take passengers along. While her children were in school, Jerrie continued to take flying lessons.

A couple of years later, she decided the time had come to get a private pilot's license. With a private pilot's license there would be fewer restrictions than with a solo permit. She would be able to take passengers along and she could fly for longer distances. In 1958, she met all the requirements, and she passed her test to finally get her private pilot's license. To celebrate her accomplishment, she flew her plane from Port Columbus to Newark-Heath airport and picked up two very special passengers, her mom and sister Susan. Susan's eyes sparkled as she recalled the big day. "I still remember how exciting it was," she said. "And I wasn't scared at all."[6]

Russ got his private pilot's license on the same day as Jerrie. To celebrate their achievement, the couple took a vacation and flew to St. Pierre, a French island in the northwestern Atlantic Ocean near Canada. In the hotel dining room, Jerrie heard pilots communicating their positions over the Atlantic from the radio room. It sounded so exciting that she vowed to Russ that one day she would fly an airplane over the ocean.

Owing to her knowledge of airplanes and flying, Jerrie managed Price Field airport in 1961, making her the first woman to manage an airport in the state of Ohio. In 1962, Russ and Jerrie Mock, along with a friend, Alfred J. Baumeister, purchased a single-engine Cessna 180. Russ used the plane mainly for business trips, but Jerrie entered a woman's race the same year they purchased it. Unfortunately, Jerrie came in last place. She explained, "I took a friend along and she was afraid. She had a panic attack, and I had to take her back, and let her out of the plane. She calmed down, and we took off again, but it added an extra hour to my flight."[7]

One night, up to her elbows in dishwater at the kitchen sink, Jerrie complained about how bored she was being a housewife and doing the same thing over and over again, day after day. "Maybe you should get in your plane and fly around the world," Russ said mockingly. "All right," she responded. "I will."[8]

Jerrie mentioned to Baumeister that she would like to fly the Cessna around the world. Baumeister agreed to the idea, but later admitted that he thought she was joking. But Jerrie never joked when it came to flying. She decided the odds were in her favor, and when she discovered that no woman had yet flown around the world, she set out to follow her childhood dream.

Their friend, Alfred Baumeister, was also a co-worker of Jerrie's husband at Bell Sound. While putting in a sound system at Lockbourne Air Force Base, he met Brigadier General Dick Lassiter. He told Lassiter about Jerrie's idea to fly around the world. Lassiter agreed to "unofficially" help her plan a route, and to get **clearances** when needed. In a top-secret room in the Pentagon, General Lassiter and Jerrie Mock mapped out a route around the world. Major Arthur C. Weiner of the United States Air Force also helped Jerrie by studying weather reports and drawing twenty-four flight plans for different legs of the flight. Amelia Earhart took along navigator Fred Noonan in her airplane; Jerrie Mock took along the flight plans of navigator Art Weiner.[9] Some of the flight maps drawn by Major Weiner were almost ten feet in length and had to be folded accordion-style so they could be stored in the cramped cockpit.

Cablegrams were sent back and forth, asking countries to allow Jerrie to land at certain airports or air force bases. Some countries just didn't want her. Jerrie wrote letters and visited **consulates** all over Washington, D.C., filling out paperwork to obtain the permissions needed to fly over and to land in the foreign countries along her route. Abdullah Hababi, from the embassy of Saudi Arabia, sent a cablegram granting permission to land as long as no "undesirable passengers" were aboard when she landed! After obtaining all the necessary permissions, Jerrie and General Lassiter discussed what equipment, and what additional emergency equipment, she would need to bring along.

While Jerrie was busy getting her paperwork in order, the family vacation plane was being transformed into a long-distance flier. With the words *Spirit of Columbus* emblazoned on its nose, and a shiny red-and-white paint job, *Charlie* looked ready to streak across the open skies. The eleven-year-old plane was renewed, inside and out. At the push of a switch, a brand new 225-horsepower engine rumbled under the cowling after being serviced by Continental Motors of Muskegon, Michigan. The engine was tested, dismantled, reassembled, and tested again four times. Jerrie flew to Fort Lauderdale for the installation of a long-range radio and then off to a Cessna service shop at the Wichita Municipal Airport in Kansas that specialized in long-distance and overseas flight preparation. *Charlie* was equipped with dual short-range radios, twin radio-direction finders, and other **components** found in larger airplanes. Massive metal gas tanks were strapped in, replacing three passenger seats. With cabin fuel tanks and wing fuel tanks, *Charlie* was capable of carrying 183 gallons of gas and flying 3,500 miles without a stop. Only one seat was needed. Jerrie was flying solo.

Her departure date in April 1964 was less than three months away when a National Aeronautic Association official called to tell her a pilot from California also wanted to become the first woman to fly around the world. A twenty-seven-year-old professional pilot named Joan Merriam Smith planned to follow the same route as Amelia Earhart. The NAA represents the FAI, the Fédération Aéronautique Internationale, in the United States. One rule of the FAI is that only one pilot at a time from each country can apply to make an attempt to set the same record. Jerrie had been planning her trip for over a year. She burst into action that same evening, and hopped on a plane bound for Washington, D.C. When the doors to the office of the NAA opened in the morning, Jerrie rushed in and registered to be the first woman to fly solo around the world.

JERRIE L. MOCK
2490 Bexford Place
Columbus 9, Ohio

I respectfully request permission for the following described flight within your territory:

1. Name of applicant: __Geraldine L. Mock, 2490 Bexford Pl., Columbus 9,__ __Ohio, U.S.A.__

2. Country and Registration No. of airplane:__ U.S.A. N-1538-C __

3. Make and Model of airplane: _____Cessna 180_____

4. Name and address of owner: __Russell C. Mock, 2490 Bexford Pl, Columbus,__ __Ohio; Alfred J. Baumeister, Wenwood Rd., Columbus, Ohio.__

5. Purpose of flight: __Pleasure flight around world.__

6. CREW INFORMATION:

   Name: __Geraldine L. Mock__

   Nationality:_____U.S.A.__

   Duties on Board:__Captain__

   License # and type: __Private, Instrument, No.__

   Expiration date license:__none__

   Passport: __EO96532__ __(U.S.A.)__

7. Passenger & Cargo information: _____None__

8. Origin of flight: _____Columbus, Ohio U.S.A.__

9. Ultimate destination: ____Columbus, Ohio, U.S.A.__

10. Airport of landing your country:_____

11. Point of penetration your boundries: _____

12. Route of flight within your boundries:_____

13. Point of departure your boundries:_____

14. Radio communication frequencies:_____

15. Amount of third party liability insruance carried: __$1,000,000 (U.S.)__

16. Name of company covering insurance: __Lloyds__

Any cooperation that you can give me in the issuance of landing or overflight permits will be greatly appreciated.

Very truly yours,

Geraldine L. Mock

JERRIE MOCK'S APPLICATION FOR LANDING RIGHTS IN VARIOUS COUNTRIES DURING HER SOLO TRIP AROUND THE WORLD

Susan Reid collection

SINGLE-ENGINE VERSUS
TWIN-ENGINE PLANES

JERRIE MOCK was asked over and over again about her choice to fly around the world in a single-engine airplane. After all, she would be traveling great distances over deserts and oceans. Jerrie explained that a single-engine plane uses less gas and can fly for a longer distance before needing to refuel. With better fuel mileage she would need to carry less fuel and her plane would be lighter. Charles Lindbergh also believed a small single-engine plane was the best choice when he flew across the Atlantic Ocean. He figured that with two engines there was twice the chance of one failing. With a twin-engine plane both engines must be maintained and monitored.

Jerrie Mock explained to a *Columbus Dispatch* reporter:

From the point of safety it must be understood that the typical light twin is not a single-engine with a spare engine . . . it is a two-engine airplane. True, a light twin-engine airplane will maintain **altitude** . . . even climb modestly on one engine. But only if not heavily loaded. During much of my hops I would be in a little better shape, if any, if I were in a light twin in an engine-out condition than if I lose an engine on my 180, I'd go down.[10]

But to make a trip around the world, an airplane would need to be loaded with supplies and emergency equipment. At times, the plane would need to haul a full load of fuel. The average light twin-engine plane isn't good at maintaining altitude when it's loaded down. So, during times of engine failure Jerrie would be better off in a twin-engine plane, but at all other times the single-engine plane was the best pick.

Without an official permit, Joan Merriam Smith still wanted to be the first to complete that flight. Joan left from California on March 17 to follow Amelia Earhart's route. That same day, Jerrie rushed to Kansas to get *Charlie* out of the factory to be ready for her new departure date of Thursday, March 19. What began as a leisurely trip to circle the globe suddenly became a race around the world!

DID YOU KNOW?

Orville and Wilbur Wright were credited with inventing the first airplane. On December 17, 1903, the two brothers piloted the first powered and controlled airplane flight near Kitty Hawk, North Carolina. Orville flew 120 feet in twelve seconds, while Wilbur soared 852 feet in fifty-nine seconds.

During their four years of effort, the brothers took five roundtrip train rides from Dayton, Ohio, to Kitty Hawk. They endured horrific storms, ridicule, and disappointment after disappointment. That December, Orville and Wilbur finally succeeded in making the first engine-powered flight.

FLIGHT THREE

BERMUDA BOUND

FLYING AT an altitude of 7,500 feet, Jerrie finally felt at peace, alone in her plane. She flew over mountains and marveled at the patchwork of land below her. As she flew past Richmond, Virginia, she tingled with excitement at the thought of finally living her dream of flying over the Atlantic Ocean. Jerrie reached down and released the long-distance radio antenna wire. The wire, one hundred feet long, unraveled and hung below the plane, but the radio stayed silent. Jerrie looked down at the needle on the meter. It should have been moving, searching for a signal, but it remained motionless. She leaned in closer to the meter, but all was silent. She heard nothing, not a peep.

Jerrie wondered if she needed a long-distance radio to make a safe crossing over the ocean. She had never discussed the possibility of a radio failure with Lassiter or Weiner, so she had no idea what to do. Should she land in Richmond? Should she turn back and go home? After all the planning and all the excitement, how could she possibly let so many people down? Jerrie looked down at the triangles that marked

JERRIE MOCK IS SHOWN THE NEWLY INSTALLED LONG-DISTANCE
RADIO ANTENNA

Susan Reid collection

the course on the charts of her flight plan. She was told to report at each triangle. Now what would she do? So many people were counting on her. She just couldn't turn back before she even left the country. She felt that she would rather face her first flight over the ocean without communication than to turn back and go home a failure.

Jerrie got on her short-range radio. She informed the air traffic controller that she was on the proper channel, but had no contact with New York Oceanic, one of the four major international airspaces of the United States. The controller in the tower gave her another frequency to try. Jerrie tried it, knowing all the while that it wouldn't work. Her long-range radio was dead. But communicating with the controller gave her time—time to make a decision. Would the Air Force be angry if she tried to fly over the ocean without a radio? If she told someone what was happening, would they tell her to turn back? As she considered all the pros and cons of flying without a long-range radio, the transmission to the tower nearly faded away. Jerrie's hands shook as she picked up the microphone and called the controller one last time. She told him she would call again when she was close to Bermuda. With the decision made, she took a deep breath and pointed *Charlie* over the vast blue ocean before them.

With more than a thousand miles to go, the drone of the engine comforted Jerrie as she flew in and out of clouds above the endless ocean. But she remained nervous. Jerrie had lots of concerns about flying over the Bermuda Triangle. She later wrote, "I was flying over the mysterious Bermuda Triangle, where so many ships and planes have disappeared without explanation or any trace of debris, as if they were caught in a whirlpool and pulled down in a hole in the ocean floor. . . . Remember the World War I collier, *U.S.S. Cyclops*, that vanished in clear, calm weather with never a trace? Remember the whole flights of Navy patrol planes that flew into the void, never to return?"[1] As she flew over the Bermuda Triangle, alone and without radio communication, she recalled how they had all disappeared forever, just like Amelia Earhart.

THE INSTRUMENT PANEL IN THE COCKPIT OF THE CESSNA 180,
CHARLIE

Courtesy of Phoenix Graphix

To avoid her feelings of doom and gloom, Jerrie forced herself to keep her mind on navigation. She turned on the **automatic direction finder** (ADF) in hopes of picking up a signal from the Bermuda beacon. There were two sets of needles and they pointed to different locations. Which one was giving the correct direction? She remembered how the addition of the fuel tanks made it necessary to relocate the antenna of the number two ADF while the plane was serviced in Wichita. The number one ADF hadn't been moved. With no radio and no one to talk with about the situation, she made an educated guess and followed the undisturbed ADF.

Jerrie searched for blue skies after flying in a sea of clouds for some time. She dipped down out of the cloud cover and both ADF

VISUAL FLIGHT RULES (VFR) VERSUS INSTRUMENT FLIGHT RULES (IFR)

PILOTS FLYING under **visual flight rules (VFR)** can operate an aircraft in conditions clear enough to allow them to see. VFR is regulated by distance from the clouds, a reference to the ground, and a minimum visibility. Pilots assume the responsibility to avoid obstruction and other aircraft. Pilots who seek additional training can obtain an instrument rating to fly **instrument flight rules (IFR)**. For training purposes the pilot wears **foggles**, a type of goggle that blocks the field of vision and allows the pilot to see only the instrument panel of the aircraft. With an IFR flight plan, the pilot is in constant radar contact and is governed by the air traffic controller. IFR is used in bad weather, cloud cover, and fog. Any pilot flying over eighteen thousand feet is required to use instrument flight rules.

needles spun like mad. Then, as she was heading east, the needles stopped spinning and indicated Bermuda was behind her, to the southwest. She turned the plane around, and there before her was the island of Bermuda!

She contacted the person in the control tower at Kindley Air Force Base and he recommended a **surveillance radar approach.** The man in the tower wanted to guide her in for a landing using radar. Jerrie preferred to land visually, but she was exhausted from her stressful day. Every muscle tensed as she prepared for her first landing using instruments without an instructor beside her. She followed the directions from the control tower and came in for a smooth landing.

KNOTS VERSUS MILES PER HOUR

1 **KNOT** = 1.15077945 miles per hour

Miles per hour and knots are speeds that indicate the number of units of distance covered during a certain amount of time. The speed of an aircraft is measured in knots.

1 knot = 1 nautical mile per hour = 6,076 feet per hour

1 mph =1 mile per hour = 5,280 feet per hour

For example, if a car is moving at 50 mph on a highway, how would you represent this speed in knots?

Convert the speed in miles per hour that the car is moving to the speed in feet per hour. This is accomplished by multiplying by the number of feet in a mile.

50 (mph) × 5,280 (feet/mile) = 264,000 (feet/hr)

Now, convert the feet per hour to knots by multiplying by the knots conversion factor: 1 (knot)/6,076 (feet/hr).

264,000 (feet/hr) × 1 (knot)/6,076 (feet/hr) = 43.4 knots

Once on the ground, Jerrie realized that the terminal at the airbase was still miles away. Strong winds battered the little plane as she tried to steer it to the terminal building. The wind pushed at the back end of the plane, threatening to whip the tail end around. Jerrie stood hard on the brakes, trying to keep the plane from spinning in the wind. No matter how hard she stood on the brake pedal, it wouldn't stick. Her brakes were not working! The left wheel kept rolling faster than the right. In the rush to get in the air to circle the globe before Joan Merriam Smith, could the brakes have been overlooked? Now, when she needed them the most, she realized she didn't have any brakes.

Charlie's back end whipped around and they went into a spin. After a 360-degree rotation, she let the plane roll onto the grass, hoping the friction of the grass could keep it from spinning again. A bunch of airport attendants came running out, grabbed onto the wing **struts**, and guided them in. When they finally came to a stop at the terminal, Jerrie took a deep breath and shut the plane off, almost too exhausted to open the door.

After Jerrie met with the press, Mrs. Bill Judd, the wife of a Trans World Airline captain, invited Jerrie to stay at her house since her husband was on a flight bound for Europe, and wouldn't be home for a few days. Jerrie accepted the invitation and, after a good night's rest, woke excited with anticipation about the big day ahead of her. On her list was getting the long-distance radio to work, having her brakes fixed, obtaining a weather forecast for the North Atlantic, getting gas for *Charlie*, filling out forms, and writing an article for the newspaper back home. Before even getting out of bed, she phoned the Kindley AFB for the weather forecast. The news of hurricane-strength, **gale-force** winds made her high spirits plummet. She looked out the window at the waves crashing against the rocks and she decided she had better stay grounded. Besides, there were plenty more items on her to-do list to take care of.

Jerrie hopped in a taxi and took a scenic drive along the coast to the offices of Bermuda Air Services. She was informed that Joan Merriam Smith was heading to San Juan, Puerto Rico. Jerrie needed to leave the island as quickly as possible, so she decided to have someone look at the long-distance radio, and she would worry about the brakes later. Luckily, she found a radioman who had worked at Pan American World Airways. He checked the plane and agreed that the radio was dead; he believed that the problem had to be in the wires behind the gas tank. By late afternoon, the plane was stripped of its cargo. Once the gas tanks were removed, the radioman declared, "Well, there's a wire disconnected, all right. And it just didn't come off—the raw lead is all taped up and tucked away. The radio could never work like that."[2]

So many thoughts popped into Jerrie's mind. The radio had been installed in Fort Lauderdale, Florida. It had been tested multiple times and had worked just fine. Was there someone out there who wanted her to fail? After fifty years, Jerrie Mock felt she could say what she couldn't say then: "It was sabotage!"[3]

DID YOU KNOW?

The three points of the Bermuda Triangle are Miami, Puerto Rico, and Bermuda. The first person to document strange things going on in the area of the Bermuda Triangle was Christopher Columbus. He reported mysterious lights and claimed odd things happened to his compass in this area.

FLIGHT FOUR

SANTA MARIA

JERRIE WANTED to hug the mechanic who had fixed her long-distance radio, but instead she thanked him politely. She spent the rest of the day putting the huge gas tanks back into the tiny cockpit with the help of some men at the airport. When the gas tanks were secured, the men helped her load all her belongings back into the plane. The local men had worked for two long, hard days over the weekend, and charged Jerrie only ten dollars.

The following morning, Jerrie was anxious to get back up in the air, but she awoke to Mother Nature pounding the island with another storm, keeping her grounded another day. That evening, Jerrie moved to the home of her FAI observer, John Fountain, and his family, since the Judd house was rather small, and Bill was returning from his flight. She had hoped to leave for the island of Santa Maria as soon as possible, but the storm continued to batter Bermuda.

As the days passed, Russ begged Jerrie to press on, but she ignored his pleas. He told her that Joan Merriam Smith had already taken off for South America. Jerrie explained that she was relying on the pilot reports, or PIREPS. She figured if the professionals weren't flying, neither was she. "I assured Russ I lost interest in flying the Atlantic that day when the Air Force told me they had cancelled all flights to the Azores. If those boys don't want to try it, I'm sure I don't. I am losing precious time, but I would be in worse shape if I got to Santa Maria and couldn't land or had to attempt a dangerous landing in **low ceiling** and visibility conditions. I could damage the airplane badly and really cause a delay."[1]

The Fountains kept Jerrie busy with lunches, shopping, and movies. The British family taught Jerrie how to properly serve tea. Lillian Fountain's mother, ninety-year-old Nana, treated the stranded pilot to plum pudding and other delicacies. Jerrie enjoyed her time with the Fountain family, but she longed to get back in the air, alone in her plane.

With the days nearing a week, Jerrie paced the floor of her room and walked the path to the weather station at Kindley Air Force Base over and over again. On March 26, seven days after arriving in Bermuda, she was told if she didn't leave that day, she would be grounded by incoming storms. The winds had calmed from seventy-five knots down to twenty. There would be storms, but none as severe as the ones they had endured or the ones on the way. Jerrie called Russ to tell him the good news, and he happily promised to write something for the newspaper. Jerrie packed her canvas bag, while Nana prepared sandwiches, cakes, and English pork pies for her to take along on the flight to Santa Maria. After a navigation session with Bill Judd on the use of **Consolan** stations to find her way over the ocean, Jerrie was ready for her next adventure.

Late in the afternoon of March 26, at 4:56 p.m., Jerrie Mock finally sat behind the controls of her beloved *Charlie*. She settled into her seat and informed the controller in the tower that she was ready for takeoff. The engine roared to life. After *Charlie* had climbed to nine thousand feet, Jerrie let out the trailing antenna of the long-distance radio. As she traveled the 2,100 miles to her destination of Santa Maria, voices of pilots came over the long-distance radio wishing her good luck, while

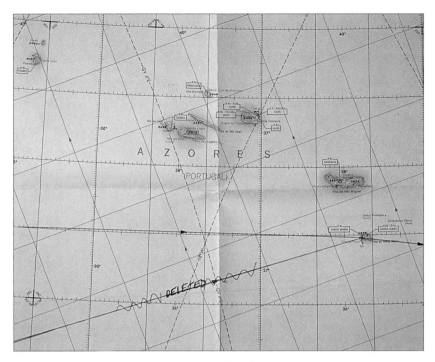

AERONAUTICAL MAP OF THE AZORES

Courtesy of Phoenix Graphix

others just said hello. Hearing their voices made her feel less lonely as she lived her dream of flying across the Atlantic Ocean.

Before darkness fell, Jerrie checked her flashlights and her map light. The sun went down, and the stars came out. She had a spectacular view of the sparkling sky. *Charlie*'s engine hummed steadily. Suddenly, *Charlie* slowed down and dropped to a lower elevation. Jerrie increased the power, but the plane kept falling. Something was terribly wrong! She shone the flashlight around the outside of the plane, and the beam of light revealed an inch of ice, clinging to the wing struts. If ice was on the struts, it was certainly on the wings. Jerrie knew that ice on a plane would destroy the smooth flow of air; it could also be deadly since the weight of the ice would reduce a plane's lift. Ice could stall a plane, stop an engine, and cause the plane to roll and pitch.

NAVIGATIONAL SYSTEMS
—THEN AND NOW

IT WASN'T until the 1970s that pilots had more accurate light-weight navigation systems in the cockpit. Long before they had GPS, or Global Positioning Systems, travelers found their way by celestial navigation, which involved watching the stars, the sun, and the moon. Jerrie Mock used a Jeppesen computer and a magnetic compass, along with maps, charts, and two ADFs, or automatic direction finders. At times she used **dead reckoning** to determine her position with information she obtained from her compass, along with time and air-speed indicators. She also relied on her ADF to pick up signals from beacons. In 1964, beacons from some stationary Navy boats emitted a signal to help airplanes find their way over the vast ocean waters. Airports also used beacons to help pilots locate them. While en route on her historic flight, Jerrie learned how to use the Consolan navigational radio system, a historical navigation system that is no longer in use today. Consolan stations sent out signals that were picked up by the ADF. The stations sent a combination of dots and dashes that always totaled fifty. Navigation was achieved by counting these signals and checking them against a special map. By monitoring two stations, Jerrie Mock could almost determine her exact location by using triangulation. Many pilots preferred to use a navigator to do all the calculations to find their way, but Jerrie preferred to fly solo.

CALL SIGNS

PLANES ARE identified by call signs, a combination of letters and numbers visible on the side of the plane. The first letter, "N," identifies the aircraft as from the United States of America. The call sign that identified Jerrie's plane was N1538C and could be shortened to Three-Eight Charlie.

Charlie had no de-icing equipment. Jerrie thought of her options. Her first thought was to descend to warmer air, but she remembered reports of storms in the lower altitudes. Her only option was to go up and hope to clear the clouds. She repeatedly requested permission to rise, but no one answered her calls. She called for clearance again and again, but still no answer. She lost more speed and more altitude. If she didn't get help soon, she was going down into the icy shark-infested waters of the Atlantic Ocean!

Finally a voice came over the radio, "November One-Three-Eight Charlie, Santa Maria. Understand you have ice, are requesting flight level one-one-zero. Is that affirmative?"

"Affirmative. Affirmative."

"Three-Eight Charlie, Santa Maria. Stand by one."[2]

Jerrie pressed on the throttle for more speed and pointed the beam of the flashlight on the plane. The ice had doubled from the first time she had looked. She worried that, by the time she got clearance, *Charlie* would be too heavy with ice to make the climb. As precious seconds became minutes, Jerrie once again got on the radio to ask for clearance to go up. Once again she was instructed to stand by. She understood they needed to check on traffic in the area, but she needed permission to change course, and she needed it now.

AERIAL VIEW OF THE ISLAND OF SANTA MARIA

Courtesy of Phoenix Graphix

Jerrie looked out at the struts. More ice. She couldn't wait one minute more! Just when she felt desperate enough to rise without clearance, she was given permission to change her course to a higher altitude. She took action. *Charlie* responded and rose safely above the clouds. Jerrie leveled the plane and said a prayer of thanks. Soon the sun came up, and its warm rays melted the ice off the struts and the wings.

She had been flying for thirteen hours when a break in the clouds exposed land, mountainous land. Jerrie contacted the tower at the Santa Maria airport. Due to the heavy cloud cover, she was told to land her plane using instruments only. The reading from her compass had not been reliable at all, so she tuned in her automatic direction finder and picked up the signal from the beacon at the airport.

The air traffic controller gave her clearance to land, but then he added, "Three-Eight Charlie. Don't hit the mountains."[3]

Jerrie couldn't believe his comment about hitting mountains. Of course she planned to avoid them! But with a welcoming runway before her, she concentrated on making a good and safe landing. As soon as *Charlie's* wheels touched the airstrip, she slowed the plane down, and headed for the terminal.

DID YOU KNOW?

There are nine islands in the North Atlantic Ocean known as the Azores. Santa Maria, the southernmost island, is thirty-eight square miles. It is believed the island was discovered by a Portuguese explorer in the early 1400s. Myth has it that one of the lookouts on the ship's crew spotted the distant island of Santa Maria while celebrating mass on the feast of the Virgin Mary, and he declared, "Santa Maria!"

On February 16, 1493, when Christopher Columbus was returning home from the West Indies, he and his crew stopped at Santa Maria. They went to mass in a small church overlooking the water. At the sight of enemy ships in the distance, the men rushed to one of their ships. In their hurry to leave, they cut the anchor before sailing home. The anchor was recovered from the sea and is now on display on the island of Santa Maria.

FLIGHT FIVE

CASABLANCA

A CROWD OF people at the Santa Maria airport greeted Jerrie. They spoke Portuguese, a clear reminder that she was really far from home, in the Azores, volcanic islands west of Portugal. Tired and stiff from sitting for more than thirteen hours, Jerrie nearly tumbled from her plane. The day was chilly and rainy, but her feet were on the ground and she felt thankful that both she and *Charlie* were in one piece after the icy flight. She posed for photos and then followed the air force representatives to the terminal building. Jerrie had been awake for twenty-four hours, so, after a snack of tropical fruit and coffee, she was taken to the only hotel on the island of Santa Maria, The Terra Nostra.

At the hotel, Jerrie wrote to the newspaper, "Airplane brakes are a weak point, and this is not serious. It won't take more than an hour or so to correct and is not too important in any event since I am using excellent airports everywhere in route."[1] When the article was finished, she plopped down onto the bed. Jerrie craved some sleep after being awake both day and night.

After a couple of hours of sleep, Jerrie woke to the sound of a piercing bell, so loud that the walls of her room trembled. She didn't know why the bell had sounded, but she was now wide awake, and too excited to go back to sleep. After all, there was an island to explore! She went to the restaurant to have some lunch and was joined by the airport manager, Alexandre Negrao. She informed him of her failing brakes, so after lunch he took her to the home of Jack Duffield, the Pan American manager, to see if he could help. Jerrie also mentioned to Duffield that her compass might be a few degrees off. Duffield told Jerrie that the small airport did not have a compass rose on the field in order to check the accuracy of the compass, but he had a mechanic at the airfield who would look at *Charlie*'s brakes. Unfortunately, the mechanic had bad news. The brakes needed to be replaced. This news puzzled Jerrie since she had understood *Charlie* had brand new brakes installed before they left Columbus. To make matters worse, there were no parts for her plane on the island. The only brakes Duffield had in stock were for a 707, a much larger airplane. His parting advice was, "Try not to hit the brakes."[2]

With no options for getting her plane repaired, Jerrie spent the rest of the day touring the mystical island. Away from the airport, Alexandre drove Jerrie down roads partly covered with fog, which wound around the mountain ranges. Oxen pulling carts traveled down the dirt roads in place of cars. Peasants trudged along the side of the road with packs on their backs. The people of the island lived off the land by growing crops in the fields and catching fish in the sea. Jerrie remembered, "Almost as Alice dropped into Wonderland, I stepped into the past. The people, their clothes, their tools, their houses, all belonged in a history book."[3] After touring the island, Jerrie went back to her room to write letters and get some rest. That evening she enjoyed dinner with Jack Duffield, her FAI observer, and members of a flying group called Wings of the Atlantic. Jerrie made certain to get a few recipes for the wonderful dishes before she left.

When dinner was over, Jerrie went to a radio station for an interview. Upon her return to the hotel, she joined some people sitting by a cozy fire in the lounge. After a while she went to her room, finished writing a letter to Russ, and fell fast asleep. The next day, she awoke to icy winds and dark skies. At the airport, she was handed a flight plan with the word, "RISK" written across it. Jerrie didn't want to postpone the flight after being delayed in Bermuda for a week, but the combination of bad brakes and high winds worried her. She didn't want to take the chance of spinning out again. After all, she had her reputation at stake, along with the reputation of "lady pilots" in general. Some airport men recommended that she take off from a large ramp that had been used for military planes. Crosswinds were blowing across the runway, and the air seemed calmer by the ramp. Jerrie agreed it was the best choice and gathered her things together for her departure.

Before Jerrie boarded her plane, Alexandre Negrao handed her sandwiches and tomato juice. He explained it was sent from Pedro, a sixteen-year-old boy she had met on the island. Jerrie appreciated the boy's kindness, and felt sad to have to leave so soon. Along with many wonderful recipes, the local people had given Jerrie a souvenir doll to take home to her little girl, Valerie. Jerrie shook her head. "My dream was to see the world, not to be the first woman to fly around it."[4] But along the way her trip had become a competition, one she wanted to win. She thought of all the folks back home, counting on her success, and boarded her tiny plane.

Jerrie buckled her seat belt, anxious to begin the one-thousand-mile flight to Casablanca. She took off down the runway and flew over choppy waters before ascending to the 9,500-feet cruising level. The fierce winds pushed *Charlie* from behind, and the plane bumped along in the stormy air. Jerrie tightened her belts and kept a keen eye on the instruments, as well as on the angry purple and orange sky. *Charlie* was set on **autopilot**, but the single-engine plane slowed. Something was not right. On autopilot, a plane goes the speed designated by the pilot. Why was *Charlie* slowing down? Jerrie looked out of the window only to realize her worst fears had come true. Once again her wing struts and wings were covered with ice.

A WEATHER MAP OF THE ROUTE FROM CASABLANCA TO BÔNE

Courtesy of Phoenix Graphix

She called the tower controller, explained her grim situation, and asked permission to go to a higher altitude. The controller calmly told her to wait. Once again, Jerrie tensed, being forced to stand by while the ice on Charlie thickened. After much back and forth, she finally was cleared to ascend to 11,500 feet, out of the freezing mist, out of danger. Her tension, along with the ice, melted in the warm sun above the clouds. Five hours later, she began her descent to Casablanca, a city of clean, white houses.

Jerrie landed at Anfa Airport and was met by a large crowd of people with armloads of flowers and plenty of photo requests. The control tower operator, Henri Richaud, helped her get through **customs**. Before they left the airport, Jerrie sat down with a group of reporters in a huge room and answered all their questions. Jerrie could understand how animals in a zoo felt by the way everyone stared at her.

Back home in Columbus, Ohio, Jerrie made front-page headlines in the local newspaper with her world-record-breaking flight. The article read, "Jerrie Mock flew into aviation history books Saturday afternoon when she completed a flight from the United States to Africa. No other woman has ever piloted a plane over this route according to the international aviation record keepers, the National Aeronautics Association in Washington, D.C. Total time in the air was twenty-five hours and fifteen minutes."[5]

While in Casablanca, Jerrie toured the city. She had pictured Africa as full of jungles and deserts, so she was surprised to see beautiful beaches. That evening, Jerrie's hosts, Henri Richaud and his wife, took her to the city to enjoy a nice dinner. Jerrie shared the story of her night out with the *Dispatch*. She wrote, "We drove through parts of the Old City with its narrow, jammed streets and passageways. We stopped at a fabulous restaurant for dinner. . . . One of the main courses was 'cartilla,' which is a poultry pie. The top layer under the crust is pigeon meal, and beneath are hunks of chicken, turkey, goose, and, I guess, various other types of food birds."[6] Dinner began with Ramadan soup, followed by the pigeon pie, and couscous. "It was wonderful," she said, "delicious and spicy."[7] The sights, the sounds, and the tasty meal made the entire evening feel like a magic carpet ride.

The following day Jerrie received a call from her husband, Russ, asking about her plans. "When are you leaving?" he asked.

"Not today. Henri just got the weather report and it's pretty bad: thunderstorms, low ceilings, icing. After flying with ice for the last two days, I don't want any more for a while."[8]

Russ confessed he had been worried about her. General Lassiter from the Pentagon, who had helped Jerrie chart her course in preparation of her journey, had been keeping Russell Mock informed of her whereabouts. Jerrie and Russ chatted for a while, and he updated her on family events. It was Easter Sunday, and they were oceans apart. She

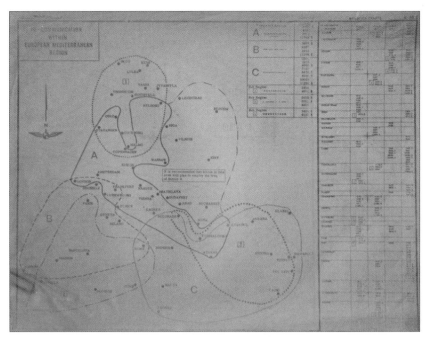

A COMMUNICATION MAP FOR THE EUROPEAN MEDITERRANEAN
REGION

Courtesy of Phoenix Graphix

sent her love to Val and the boys. After the phone call, Jerrie decided to
spend the rest of the day sightseeing. Turbaned men and veiled woman
rushed about on the city streets; some of the women rode on the backs
of motor scooters. While she strolled around the shops, Jerrie purchased
a baby doll for Valerie.

For Easter dinner that evening, Jerrie feasted on a meal of snails
and roast leg of lamb. Dancers with exotic flowing dresses, gold jewels,
and bangle bracelets performed at the Richaud house. They danced to
the melody of the flute and the tambourines. After the celebration had
ended, Jerrie wrote for the newspaper before going to bed. She described
her evening and added, "My first stop in Africa is all that you could want
for romantic atmosphere."[9]

The next day Jerrie had help with a compass swing, a method used to check the accuracy of a compass. At the airfield they had a compass rose, a design painted on a taxiway or ramp that shows all four points of a compass. The compass swing revealed that for the entire trip her compass had been ten degrees off. For the remainder of her around-the-world flight, Jerrie made a mental note to always subtract ten. She left Casablanca with a feeling that flying through Africa might have more surprises on the way.

DID YOU KNOW?

The city of Casablanca is one of the largest financial centers on the African continent. It sits on the site of the medieval town of Anfa, which was built and settled by the Berbers in the twelfth century. In the early fifteenth century, the town became a safe haven for pirates. In 1468, the Portuguese attacked the pirates and destroyed Anfa. They returned to the area in 1515 and built a new town named Casa Branca, meaning "white house" in Portuguese.

In 1755, an earthquake destroyed Casa Branca, leaving it abandoned. After its reconstruction in the late eighteenth century, the town was named Casablanca, meaning "white house" in Spanish. As Jerrie Mock approached Anfa Airport in Casablanca, she marveled at how white and clean the city looked from the air, and quickly understood the city's name.

FLIGHT SIX

NIGERIA AND LIBYA

T HE NEXT day, fifty-mile-per-hour winds, ice, and **squalls** were predicted. The trip to Tunis, the capital of Tunisia, would be nearly impossible in the little Cessna. The weather report worried Jerrie, but she needed to press on if she wanted to win the race to be the first woman to fly around the world. She spoke with Henri Richaud. "Henri, I know of pilots back home who are dead because they trusted a weather forecast. . . . If I were even familiar with the area it would help. If it weren't for the mountains I'd try, because I'm not afraid to make a 'one-eighty' if weather deteriorates. But not a 'one-eighty' into a mountain I can't see."[1]

After talking with Henri and the meteorologists, Jerrie decided that the best choice was to change course and leave for Bône, Nigeria. It was a place she had never heard of before, but the weather conditions and visibility were more favorable. Thunderstorms would be a factor, however, and she needed to leave quickly, or the weather could become too severe.

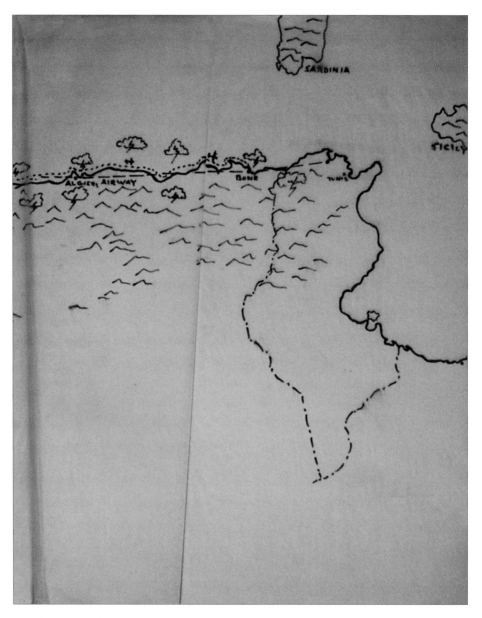

A HAND-DRAWN WEATHER MAP ALONG THE ALGIERS AIRWAY

Courtesy of Phoenix Graphix

Before leaving for Bône, Jerrie asked for her typewriter to be sent home. The cockpit was too crowded and she had never found time to write in the plane. Once the plane was refueled and the paperwork completed, Jerrie took off and flew close to land, along the shoreline. She kept her senses on high alert as she flew close to the Rif Mountains on a foggy, rainy day. She hummed the tunes to her favorite songs as she passed over Oran and Algiers, but they were just cities on a map; due to the murky weather, she saw them only in her imagination. Shortly before she arrived at Bône, a dark black thundercloud blocked her way. Lightning flashed a warning sign. After forty-five minutes of circling, she grew weary. When the storm finally moved up the coast, and out of her path, she came in for a landing. During her final approach, "the last rays of the sun broke through the cumuli and bathed the little seacoast town with its golden radiance. It was an eerie light that often comes after a storm. The white ships in the harbor, the shiny rooftops, and the emerald palms shimmered against the backdrop of a deep purple sky. The rain-swept runway was like a golden finger."[2]

After an easy landing, Jerrie took care of her plane and then set out to find some food. She found the only English-speaking man at the airport. As English was considered the official flying language, all international airports were required to have at least one employee who spoke the language. In some countries, that one controller in the field might be the only person in the town who spoke English.

The man offered to exchange her money from dollars to francs, so, once she found a restaurant, she could pay for her food. He explained that exchanging money for foreign currency was a crime in his country, and he could be sent to jail. But he felt bad for the "lady pilot." The banks were shut down for the day, and she would need francs to buy food. He agreed to exchange just enough money so she would be able to eat.

Jerrie couldn't understand how a money exchange could be a crime, but her stomach rumbled. She handed him some American dollars and he gave her the correct amount back in francs. Jerrie thanked him and left in search of a place to eat. She walked aimlessly through the dark streets and alleys. Luckily, some boys noticed the woman in Western clothes walking alone. They helped her find the way to the Café Moulin Rouge, a local French restaurant. Later, she learned the part of town she was roaming around in was so dangerous that even during World War II soldiers were instructed to always carry weapons or walk in groups when in that neighborhood![3]

Following dinner she returned to The Grand Hotel d'Orient to get some much-needed sleep. In the middle of the night, Jerrie received a frantic call from Russ, telling her that Joan Merriam Smith was covering two thousand miles a day and she needed to get moving. He couldn't understand why she was in Bône. After all, it was not on her route. Jerrie tried to explain the weather in Africa, but Russ had only one thing in his mind. He said, "Joan's on her way to Africa. Get going."[4] Jerrie slammed the receiver down. The added pressure of racing to become the first woman to fly solo around the world, on top of all the trials and tribulations she was facing daily, had become almost unbearable. It also broke her heart to hop from country to country, with so much to see, and no time to see it. After a fitful sleep, she awoke at 5:30 the next morning, put on her white "drip-dry" shirt and blue cotton skirt, and prepared herself for the flight to Cairo, Egypt.

The English-speaking man drove her to the airport and gave her a weather report along the way. He reported mild sandstorms near the cities of Tripoli and Benghazi and a bad sandstorm near Cairo. He recommended that she should change her plans and make a stop in Tripoli, since flying to Cairo would be much too dangerous. Jerrie remembered everything she had heard about flying in sandstorms. Sand could clog an engine and cause it to fail. A sandstorm could be so wicked it could peel the paint off a plane. Some had been so severe that the pilots became disoriented and, in a few cases, planes even went missing. What was good about a sandstorm? She knew Russ would want her to go all the way to Cairo, but he would have to understand. She feared running into a sandstorm more than anything Russ could have to say about Joan or anything else. "I wasn't very happy. I had never heard of 'good' sandstorms and I wondered if it might be better to take the day off and go sightseeing until they blew away. Even if the delay meant the wrath of a husband. After all, he was five thousand miles away and the sandstorms were dead ahead."[5]

With clearance to finally take off to Tripoli, Jerrie welcomed the peace of the cockpit and looked forward to the 418-mile flight. All the decision-making had made her hungry. She ate a food bar and washed it down with some water. She looked down at the vast, desolate terrain and imagined caravans of camels plodding along and wondered if they still delivered spices, gems, and ivories to trade in Tripoli. Her daydream quickly turned into a nightmare when a strange smell filled the cockpit. She sniffed again. Something was burning, and it looked like it was coming from behind the gas tank! The motor of the high-frequency radio churned. Had she actually left it on? She quickly turned the switch. The motor stopped cranking, but the smell remained. Thoughts raced through her head. She was surrounded by high-octane aviation fuel. She had to do something, but what?

Her first instinct was to land the plane, so she reached for the throttle to slow down. But a bumpy landing could cause an explosion. Even a safe landing in the desert could create sparks and spell certain death. Jerrie pushed back in her seat as fear held her in its clutch. Visions of plane crashes flashed in her mind. She remembered stories of the bomber *Lady Be Good*. In 1943, during World War II, the plane had crashed over the Libyan Desert. Fifteen years later, *Lady Be Good* and the skeletal remains of eight of its nine crewmen were finally found.

The smell of burning wires filled the cabin. "My mind flapped like a frightened bird caught in a net. Crazy fears flew at me; wild ideas about landing the plane stormed my mind. I told myself to relax. I couldn't."[6]

She looked at the door and thought about jumping, but her parachute was out of reach. Besides, if she jumped she would have to survive the desert, where the temperature of the sand could reach 140 degrees. In those extremes, she'd only survive eight to ten hours. Just the thought of it made her sweat. But what could she do? The radio was clearly out of order, so she couldn't put out a distress call. The burning wires were behind the tank, and there was no way she could reach them. She felt breathless and dizzy. Jerrie shook her head. She needed to think good thoughts. She needed to pray. She took a few deep breaths and repeated the words of the twenty-third Psalm of the Holy Bible over and over again until a peaceful feeling flowed through her.

Finally, the smell of burning insulation and wires cleared. The sun shone and *Charlie* hummed along as if nothing had happened. Jerrie said a prayer of thanks, thankful to be alive.

With a clear day and great visibility, Jerrie had a smooth landing in Tripoli. The airport was like a ghost town, and for once no one was around to greet her. When she made her way to the terminal, she learned no one from the Bône airport had sent the flight plan to Tripoli, and so the airport staff was not expecting her. She had hoped to gas up in Tripoli and continue on to Cairo, Egypt, but, after learning of more reports of severe sandstorms, she decided to spend the night. After the morning she had endured, she needed rest and a little relaxation. She checked in with customs and other officials and left the airport to spend the day sightseeing. Always the lady, respecting the customs of other countries, she changed out of her "flying skirt" into her "on-the-ground dress."[7]

Hoping to take in some local sights, Jerrie ducked down the sandy alleyways of the city. Women passed by wearing what appeared to be white sheets. They held the material over their nose with one hand, and with the other hand they held the front together. With both hands occupied, they carried everything on their heads. The shy women averted their glances, while the men bullied her. Jerrie went down one alley and a passing man bumped into her, sending her flying into a stall in the marketplace. When one fellow tried to run her over on his horse, Jerrie decided to end her shopping trip early.

Back at the hotel, Jerrie met an American woman who told her that the men in Libya didn't like women who weren't dressed in tradi-

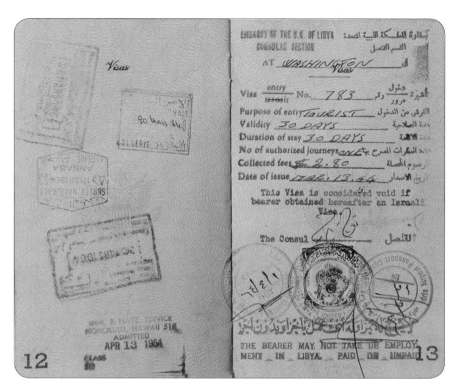

JERRIE'S PASSPORT WITH VISA STAMP FOR LIBYA

Susan Reid collection

tional robes that completely covered their heads and bodies. She added that, to respect the customs of the country, she didn't drive a car. Jerrie spent the rest of the day and the evening visiting other Americans at the hotel. Some of the men advised her to follow the coastline to Cairo. They said that they felt more comfortable flying over the desert than over the Gulf of Sirte. Jerrie politely listened to their advice, but just the thought of flying over deserts made her sweat. She decided right then and there that flying over the Gulf of Sirte was the route for her and *Charlie*.

Jerrie was rushing from country to country, unaware that Joan Merriam Smith had been stranded in Surinam. Joan had been held up for eight days. She had to wait patiently while the mechanics worked to repair a leaky gas tank. Jerrie had landed in Bône on the same day Joan finally headed to Brazil.

> *Western Union Telegram*
> *March 31, 1964*
>   *Families and sponsors scared to death because no word from you all day after landing in Tripoli. Air Force spent hours locating you from this end. Your mother in tears. Love, Russ*[8]

DID YOU KNOW?

In 1964, Libya had two capital cities, Tripoli and Benghazi. On September 1, 1969, a coup led by Muammar Gaddafi overthrew King Idris of Libya. When the Libyan Arab Republic was formed, Tripoli became the only capital of the country.

EGYPT AND SAUDI ARABIA

On April 1, Jerrie Mock finally found herself in the sky, bound for Egypt, the land of the pharaohs. Excitement built inside her as she got closer and closer to the ancient lands she had only dreamed about as a young child growing up in Newark, Ohio. She had flashbacks of images from her geography book, picturing men in flowing robes traveling by camel, trudging through the hot desert sand. Maybe, just maybe, she could find the time to ride a camel across the Sahara Desert.

After flying more than seven hours, she was cleared by the tower controller in Cairo to land on runway five. As soon as *Charlie*'s wheels touched the ground, the voice of the controller asked where she was. Wasn't she on the ground? Wasn't she at the Cairo airport? How could he not see her?

Jerrie veered her plane off the runway so she could come to a stop to figure out why she seemed to be invisible. She called the control tower again, then, right at that moment, three trucks barreled down the runway. Uniformed military soldiers surrounded *Charlie*. The men jumped out and waved their guns around. One of the soldiers told Jerrie to turn off her airplane. She turned off the engine and opened the door.

The man stepped forward, poked his head inside the cockpit, and politely said in perfect English, "Madam, you are not in Cairo."[1]

Although the sight of the soldiers and their guns terrified her, she didn't want them to sense her fear. She thrust a chart at the soldier by the plane and asked him to show her where she was on the map.

Instead of pointing out where she was, he shoved the map back at Jerrie and ordered her to follow him. Forced to leave *Charlie* behind in the custody of two soldiers, Jerrie was escorted to an air force officer's club; a building that she later learned had once been the palace of King Farouk of Egypt. Jerrie followed the soldiers into a massive hallway with a broad, tiled staircase on each side. She looked at the empty and barren rooms, and imagined how regal the palace had once looked when oriental carpets had covered the floors and beautiful thick draperies had framed the windows. She sat at a small table on the terrace, alongside a waterless swimming pool, sipping cider and tea. She explained that she was expected in Cairo, and people were waiting for her arrival, but she was told to sit and wait.

Men dressed in khaki uniforms snuck down the hallway to peek into the room where she sat. They seemed amazed at this "lady pilot" who had just landed in her plane. They wanted to know where she was headed, while Jerrie desperately wanted to know where she was. Her location remained a mystery for a while, but eventually she discovered that she had mistakenly landed at a "top secret" air force base called Inchas. They questioned her for hours until she began to wonder if they thought she was a spy!

Jerrie wanted to leave this place, and get on with her journey. She needed to eat and she needed to sleep, but most of all she needed to get to Cairo. They were expecting her! She remembered that her NAA observer was a retired Egyptian Air Force general. He would be waiting for her in Cairo. Maybe he could help? Then suddenly the air force commander came in and announced, "OK, madam. Now you can go to Cairo."[2]

Before she boarded her plane, the officer told Jerrie not to land at the military airport on her left, but to look to her right for the lights of the Cairo airport. Once Jerrie sat behind the controls, she tuned her high-frequency radio to the radio beacon coming from Cairo, to be certain not to land at yet another military base.

The stress of the unexpected landing and all the commotion that had followed had her so exhausted she could hardly think. She focused on landing her plane, hoping to get a more welcome reception when she finally arrived at Cairo International Airport. Her wish came true. A crowd of people cheered for the long-awaited "lady pilot" as she approached the terminal. Jerrie got out of her plane and went through the motions of posing for photos, answering questions, and giving autographs. In a trancelike state, she looked after *Charlie*, took care of all the necessary paperwork, and sent a story to the Columbus paper. She ordered brakes and a new antenna motor even though her brain felt clouded and muddled from exhaustion. A couple from the American embassy, Mr. and Mrs. Peter Barker, greeted Jerrie and offered to host the weary pilot in their home. Jerrie accepted their kind offer, relieved to enjoy a nice dinner and a warm bed after such a challenging day.

Jerrie awoke the following morning to the sound of chirping birds and the smell of fresh-brewed coffee. After breakfast, Peter Barker took her to the airport to make all the necessary arrangements to depart for Dhahran, Saudi Arabia, the next day. She scheduled a flight plan, checked with the weatherman, and made sure her plane was refueled. With all the paperwork complete, she was ready for some sightseeing. She knew she should get back in the air, but she was standing on the land she had dreamt about from textbooks back in grade school. Today, she would take in all the sights and sounds of this exotic land. She'd make up the time somehow, someway.

With the Barkers as her tour guides, Jerrie went across the Nile River, and traveled to the Great Pyramid of Giza, one of the Seven Wonders of the World. The three were greeted in the parking lot by camel drivers dressed in colorfully striped galabiyas, loose cotton nightshirts. Thrilled at the sight of the first camel she had seen outside of a circus or a zoo, Jerrie climbed aboard the smelly animal and rode down a twisting trail beside endless sand dunes. By the time she arrived at the pyramids, she decided that she would rather fly in a plane for ten hours than sit for thirty minutes on a camel. Jerrie wrote about the camel ride, "It is easy to see why the airplane is replacing them."[3]

At the end of the path, Jerrie found herself looking at the giant Sphinx and the 4,500-year-old Pyramid of Cheops, things she had only dreamt about visiting. Jerrie stood silent, as if under some kind of ancient magical spell. She stared at the scene before her, trying to etch it in her mind, in hopes of keeping the memory forever.

Later in the day they stopped by the Muski Bazaar, a bazaar so large it would take days to see everything. There were merchants from all over the world selling jewelry, spices, perfume, pottery, dolls, exotic outerwear, and brass, gold, and silver. After picking out a souvenir for each of the members of her family, Jerrie went to a tailor to purchase a galabiya of her own. She also found a brass lamp she could not resist, and had it shipped to her home in Ohio. That evening a reception was held in Jerrie's honor at the Aero Club. She and the Barkers gathered around a television set, sipping tea, to watch a rerun of the *Spirit of Columbus* landing at the Cairo Airport the night before.

The following day, April 3, Jerrie awoke to the sound of roosters crowing at 3:30 a.m. When she arrived at the airport, the immigration representative would not let her through because she didn't have a ticket. She tried to explain that she didn't need a ticket because she flew in on her own plane. He must have thought she had lost her mind because he kept repeating, "Lady, get out of here. I'm busy. Go buy a ticket." General Attia, her NAA observer and a retired air force general, came to her rescue, speaking in Arabic to explain the situation to the immigration man.[4]

THE SEVEN WONDERS OF
THE ANCIENT WORLD

IN 120 BCE, a Greek poet called Antipater of Sidon listed seven awe-inspiring buildings and structures that amazed him. They are known as The Seven Wonders of the Ancient World. All the "wonders" can be found in a small region around the eastern Mediterranean. The Great Pyramid of Giza is the only one that still remains. The pyramid is a tomb, a royal burial place built in an ancient cemetery at Giza in the country of Egypt. Some archeologists believe it may have taken over 100,000 men to build it. They used more than 2 million stone blocks, each weighing over 4,000 pounds. The mummified body of the great pharaoh, King Khufu, known to the Greeks as Cheops, was placed in a burial chamber deep inside his pyramid. More pyramids were built around it for King Khufu's son and grandson as well as smaller pyramids for their queens.

The Seven Wonders of the Ancient World are:

1. The Great Pyramid at Giza.

2. The Hanging Gardens of Babylon: King Nebuchadnezzar II, King of Babylon, had a beautiful garden built with every tree imaginable for his homesick young wife to remind her of her Persian roots.

3. The Temple of Artemis at Ephesus: King Croesus built the grand temple in honor of Artemis, the goddess of the moon and of the hunt, and a protector of animals and young girls.

4. The Statue of Zeus at Olympia: A famous Athenian sculptor, Phidias, was chosen to create the forty-three-foot-high statue in honor of the god Zeus.

5. The Mausoleum at Halicarnassus: Queen Artemisia built a massive tomb in Turkey as a tribute to her deceased husband and brother, King Mausolus.

6. The Colossus of Rhodes: A giant statue of the Greek titan-god of the sun Helios stood at the port city of Rhodes, on the Greek island of the same name, in the Aegean Sea off present-day Turkey.

7. The Pharos of Alexandria: The first lighthouse in the world was almost 450 feet tall; its beacon was created by fire. A huge amount of wood was needed to keep the fires lit.

A CROWD AWAITS JERRIE'S ARRIVAL AT THE DHAHRAN INTER-
NATIONAL AIRPORT IN SAUDI ARABIA

Courtesy of Phoenix Graphix

Jerrie settled behind the controls of her beloved *Charlie* and flew over the blue-green waters of the Gulf of Suez en route to Saudi Arabia. She followed a black pipeline, an area that wasn't so desolate, so if her plane went down she could be rescued. She flew over clusters of villages and many watering holes with animals gathered about. An hour into the trip, she found herself feeling dizzy. As she looked around, she noticed things had lost their shape and appeared to be blurry. She took out the oxygen mask, hoping to clear her head. Everything remained out of focus. She wiped her sunglasses. Suddenly it became clear to her that she was in the middle of a sandstorm. The only advice she had ever received about sandstorms was to avoid them. But it was too late for that. This hadn't been on the weather report—not a mention of it. She thought of landing the plane and waiting for it to clear but the ground below seemed to be moving. With the use of her instruments, she kept *Charlie* on course, and flew right through the blinding storm.

MEMBERS OF THE ROYAL ARABIAN AIR FORCE GREET JERRIE AT
THE DHAHRAN INTERNATIONAL AIRPORT

Courtesy of Phoenix Graphix

Finally the sky cleared, the sun shone, and a majestic airport came
into view. Jerrie looked down at the marble columns of the Dhahran
International Airport and felt in awe of its regal beauty. She landed on
the concrete runway and came to a stop. Hundreds of white-robed men
surrounded the plane. In Saudi Arabia, it was illegal for a woman to
drive a car, but there were no laws about woman pilots.

As soon as Jerrie climbed out of the cockpit, she was handed an
armful of flowers. Members of the Royal Arabian Air Force, sent on behalf of King Faisal, greeted Jerrie. A man in the crowd eagerly pushed his
way past the guards to sneak a look into the cockpit. After seeing nothing but huge gasoline tanks and only one seat, he turned and shouted,
"There is no man!" The crowd erupted with a "rousing ovation."[5]

CHARLIE AT THE BEAUTIFUL DHAHRAN INTERNATIONAL AIRPORT

Courtesy of Phoenix Graphix

DID YOU KNOW?

The Israeli army made a surprise attack against Egypt's air-fields on June 5, 1967. The Six-Day War virtually destroyed the Egyptian Air Force on the ground, including the top-secret Egyptian Air Force base called Inchas. Jerrie wondered if the palace or any of the men she had met that night had survived the blast. She had accidentally arrived on the air-strip at Inchas on April 1, 1964, and has since called it her April fool's landing.

FLIGHT EIGHT

PAKISTAN
AND INDIA

J ERRIE WOKE feeling refreshed, ready for the next stop on her journey, Karachi, Pakistan. She pointed *Charlie*'s nose out over the Persian Gulf, toward Bahrain Island, a place where Marco Polo had once
wandered. About an hour from her destination, she heard a voice from
the control tower, "November One-Five-Three-Eight Charlie, PIA Oh-
Five Karachi requests your occupation."

Puzzled by the request, Jerrie asked him to repeat the question. Once
again she was asked her occupation. She answered, "PIA Seven-Oh-
Five, this is November One-Three-Five-Eight Charlie. If you want my
occupation, it's a housewife."[1] The radio went silent for a bit before he
thanked her for the answer. Why would they ask such a question? She
had already been labeled "the flying housewife" back home. Jerrie had
never liked it; she only wished to be respected as an able pilot, with no
references to her gender or her occupation. Jerrie rolled her eyes and
took another look at her charts as she flew along the shoreline of the
Arabian Sea, to Karachi, the largest city in Pakistan.

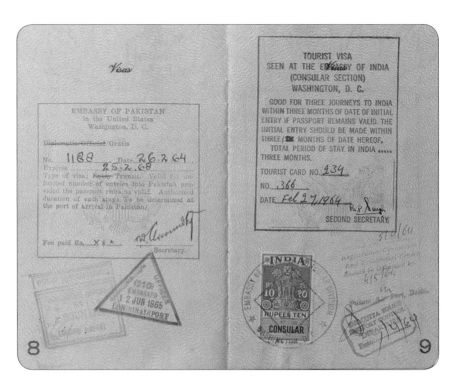

JERRIE'S PASSPORT WITH VISA STAMPS FOR PAKISTAN AND INDIA
Susan Reid collection

Jerrie exited her plane and greeted the crowd that had assembled. The women wore colorful silk **saris** and dainty pantaloons, a stark contrast to the women in Saudi Arabia, a country where ladies hid under a full body covering and observed the world through slits in their black veils. After securing her plane, Jerrie was invited to stay with John and Adelaide Tinker from the American embassy. Adelaide had much in common with Jerrie, as she too was a pilot.

While en route to the Tinkers' apartment, the three wove through streets filled with bicycles, **rickshaws**, cars, trucks, and camels pulling carts. Once inside, Jerrie settled into her room. One window overlooked the Arabian Sea and the other window had a view of the Gulf of Oran. She sat down by a window to write and to enjoy the beautiful scenery.

JERRIE IS GREETED BY JOHN TINKER FROM THE U.S. EMBASSY
AND HIS WIFE, ADELAIDE TINKER, UPON ARRIVING IN KARACHI,
PAKISTAN

U.S. government photo

After finishing a letter to her mom, she wrote an article to send to her hometown newspaper.

That evening, Jerrie enjoyed an appetizer of **caviar** (fish eggs), followed by a steak dinner. After dark, her host invited her up on the rooftop, to a small observatory and a music room. As local stringed instruments played, Jerrie looked through a telescope at a sky full of stars sparkling brightly in the desert sky. While on the rooftop, they discussed Joan Merriam Smith. Pakistan was the only point where the two pilots' routes had crossed, and the Tinkers had planned on asking Joan to stay with them when she arrived. They had learned that she was thought to be in Africa, and should be landing in Karachi in a couple of days. Jerrie did the math in her head. Joan had left two days before she did, but Joan's trip ended in California, not in Ohio. Once Jerrie landed in America, she had a lot of land to cover to get back to the **Buckeye State**. Jerrie knew one thing and one thing for sure. She needed to leave for Delhi, India, first thing in the morning!

Early the next day, Jerrie was greeted at the Karachi airport by Shukria Ali, Pakistan's most famous woman flyer. Shukria arrived wearing silk pants and a brightly colored top. Jerrie admired the trousers, and hoped the style would catch on in America, so she would no longer have to deal with skirts and stockings. Fair weather was predicted for the next leg of her trip. Shukria and Adelaide gave Jerrie some last-minute preflight instructions. Jerrie listened, amazed at how she had just left Saudi Arabia, a country in which women weren't permitted to drive, and, after only seven-and-a-half hours of flying, had arrived in Pakistan, where women wore trousers and flew planes! Just before her departure, Jerrie was given a small brass dinner-gong as a gift, so she would always remember her days in Pakistan.

Jerrie took off for India on April 5, the day before Joan Merriam Smith was scheduled to land at the Karachi airport. Back in Ohio, Jerrie had tried to prepare for her visit to India by learning to speak the language. She had asked some Indian students from the Ohio State University if they could teach her. They looked amused and said, "Okay, which one of the forty **dialects** would you like to study first?"[2] They added that the common language of the country is English, so that people from different regions could talk to each other.

After a four-and-a-half-hour flight through beautiful blue skies, Jerrie Mock landed at Palam Airport in Delhi. Newsmen asked the usual questions and well-wishers wanted to take photos with the woman pilot. Jerrie answered their questions and posed for pictures. S. C. Sen, a member of the Aero Club of India, welcomed Jerrie. He had met Amelia Earhart in 1937 when she stopped at Delhi during her attempt to fly around the world. The Cessna dealer, K. M. Raha, who had worked on Amelia's airplane, also greeted Jerrie when she landed.

Colonel G. V. Raja and his ten-year-old son offered to take Jerrie sightseeing in Delhi. Before the outing, Jerrie tried to send a cable home,

MR. & MRS. JOHN TINKER
AMERICAN EMBASSY
A.P.O. 271
NEW YORK, NEW YORK

Karachi, Pakistan
April 5, 1964

Dear Mr. Mock,

Jerrie took off this morning about 8:30 local time for Delhi. She arrived last evening about 4:00 and was received by the local press + radio.

She looked fine, and stepped out of the plane smiling and relaxed. After interviews, attending to details about getting minor repairs done, and going thru customs, she came home with us. Only a few people stopped by to welcome + congratulate her. Otherwise we tried to see she had the rest she requested.

We are amazed at how much she is expected to do. Communications in this part of the world are very poor. Sometimes it takes days to make a long distance phone call. The red tape at each stop is tedious and time consuming, besides being different in each country. Officials here were very confused about her. They had never heard of a woman flying into the country alone. She has many funny experiences to relate.

You can be very proud of her for doing a really professional job as a flier, being charming and feminine (as expected by the males) and saying the right things to the right people.

We were very pleased to have had the opportunity to share in a small way in her tremendous experience. Our thoughts and best wishes go with a gallant lady.

Sincerely, Adelaide Tinker

ADELAIDE TINKER'S LETTER TO RUSSELL, IN WHICH SHE WROTE OF JERRIE, "YOU CAN BE VERY PROUD OF HER FOR DOING A REALLY PROFESSIONAL JOB AS A FLIER, BEING CHARMING AND FEMININE (AS EXPECTED BY THE MALES), AND SAYING THE RIGHT THINGS TO THE RIGHT PEOPLE"

Susan Reid collection

but first she needed to find money to pay for it. "I got out my billfold to see what cash I had. Lots of American dollars, some pounds and shillings from Bermuda, some Portuguese escudos, some Egyptian pounds, and a few Pakistani rupees. But the man wanted Indian rupees. I didn't have any of those."[3] Colonel Raja offered to pay for the cable, but Jerrie wasn't sure how she could repay him. She decided not to send the cable and left for her tour of the city.

The first stop was Jantar Mantar, an astronomical observatory consisting of a group of massive pink-and-white concrete structures built in 1724. Its tallest **sundial** stands fifty feet in height and gives the local time, while the remaining sundials tell the time from locations in other parts of the world. From there, they went to Qutab Minar, an ornate tower of red sandstone and marble. It was called the "Victory Tower" since it was built to celebrate the Muslim defeat of Delhi's last Hindu kingdom. Jerrie and the Rajas also viewed the Iron Pillar, a pure iron shaft about twenty feet high. In its fifteen hundred years, the tower showed no sign of rust. One emperor had the Iron Pillar taken down to see why it didn't rust, but the mystery remained. Originally the pillar had swayed, and the Hindus called it *dilli,* meaning "it wobbled." Later it was firmly secured in the courtyard. Teenagers could be seen standing with their backs to the Iron Pillar while wrapping their arms around it because, legend had it, if their fingers touched they would have good luck. (Today, a protective barrier keeps tourists and teenagers at a distance.)

The tour ended at the Tomb of Humayun, built by the first wife of Mughal Emperor Humayun, Hamida Banu Begum. She started the project in 1565; it was completed in 1572.

When the sun had set that evening, the Aero Club of India held a festive party on the terrace under the stars. Jerrie enjoyed the delicious food and the people she met. One man from the press handed Jerrie a cable that read: "Please report on the sad progress of Joan Merriam Smith."[4] Jerrie had to disappoint the gentleman, because the truth was she had no idea where Joan was.

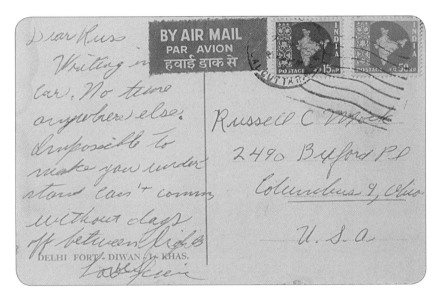

Dear Russ

Writing in car. No time anywhere else. Impossible to make you understand can't comm without clag off between flight

DELHI FORT- DIWAN -I- KHAS.

Russell C [illegible]
2490 Buford P.P
Columbus 4, Ohio
U. S. a.

THE POSTCARD THAT JERRIE SENT TO RUSSELL WHILE SHE WAS IN DELHI, INDIA

Susan Reid collection

Following the reception, Jerrie was invited to the home of Colonel Raja for some authentic Indian food and hospitality. As it was customary in India for multigenerational families to live together, at Colonel Raja's home, Jerrie met his mom, dad, aunts, uncles, sisters, and cousins. There was room for everyone and they all got along with each other. Jerrie joined in a feast of curries and other Indian foods. The Raja family smiled as they watched the stranger try all their traditional dishes. Jerrie wished she could stay longer in the home of this friendly, happy clan, but she needed to get back in her plane—the sooner, the better. She needed to stay ahead of Joan Merriam Smith.

DID YOU KNOW?

The buses in Karachi did not stop. They merely slowed down for passengers to jump on and off. If a jump was poorly timed, it could result in many broken bones!

THAILAND AND THE PHILIPPINES

TELEGRAMS FROM Russell Mock poured into the embassy; all with the same message: "Hurry home." Russ urged Jerrie to chase after her place in the history books, and neglected to inform her that Joan Merriam Smith had been held up. Due to bad weather and a revolution in Brazil, Joan could not leave that country for five days.

Jerrie boarded her plane and set out for Calcutta. She had hoped that soon after takeoff she might get a glimpse of the world famous Taj Mahal, but the beautiful tomb was in a closed air space in which she was not allowed to fly. After about a five-and-a-half-hour flight, she touched down on the runway of the Dum Dum Airport. She was still in the country of India, but she felt as if she had landed in another world. After leaving behind the pleasant weather of Delhi, Calcutta felt like a piping-hot steam room. By the time she reached the terminal, the thick air had Jerrie drenched in sweat. The overwhelming heat made her feel ill as she posed for pictures. All she wanted was a cold drink and a shower.

After all the photos were taken and the paperwork was filled out, some members of the Aero Club invited Jerrie to a gathering. While everyone else sipped hot tea on the torrid day, Jerrie requested a cold cup of tea. As she sipped her beverage, her hosts wanted to talk about Joan Merriam Smith and her whereabouts. Rumors had floated about that Joan was having mechanical problems and weather difficulties. Given that information, Jerrie realized that Joan was not going to get to Pakistan as soon as she had hoped.

While the others discussed Joan's mechanical problems, Jerrie worried about her own. *Charlie* still needed its brakes repaired, but because a plane lands against the wind, and *Charlie* was a light plane, it slowed down naturally along the runway. What she needed most was a motor for the radio's long-distance antenna, but none were available.

Jerrie went to the Lalit Great Eastern Hotel to relax in an air-conditioned room. An American woman named Mrs. Roy stopped by, along with her daughter-in-law and grandchildren, to escort Jerrie on a shopping trip among the local bazaars. Jerrie admired the colorful saris worn by the women. After purchasing some jewelry and a sari of her own, Jerrie returned to her room and collapsed. Her 3:30 a.m. wake-up call came all too soon.

Jerrie was driven to the Dum Dum Airport so she could leave Delhi and head to Bangkok, Thailand. At such an early hour, Jerrie expected the rest of the population of Calcutta to be sound asleep, but she never expected to see so many sleeping in the streets. She recalls, "Sleeping all over the place! Hundreds of them. Whole families were stretched out side by side, for block after block, on the sidewalks. In some places they were wedged so close together I doubt they could move without waking those on either side."[1] Entire families filled streets, without a home, and without hope. Some awoke from their slumber and washed in the public water fountains. The helplessness of the men, women, and children upset Jerrie. It saddened her, and the sadness was life-changing.[2] Jerrie had never known such poverty existed, and, from that moment on, she knew that she would always be a more compassionate person.

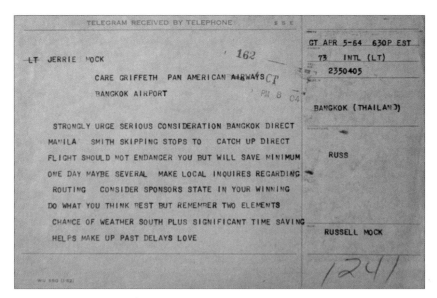

TELEGRAM RECEIVED BY TELEPHONE

GT APR 5-64 630P EST

LT JERRIE MOCK

162

73 INTL (LT)

CARE GRIFFETH PAN AMERICAN AIRWAYS CP

2350405

BANGKOK AIRPORT

PM 8 04

BANGKOK (THAILAND)

STRONGLY URGE SERIOUS CONSIDERATION BANGKOK DIRECT
MANILA SMITH SKIPPING STOPS TO CATCH UP DIRECT
FLIGHT SHOULD NOT ENDANGER YOU BUT WILL SAVE MINIMUM
ONE DAY MAYBE SEVERAL MAKE LOCAL INQUIRES REGARDING
ROUTING CONSIDER SPONSORS STATE IN YOUR WINNING
DO WHAT YOU THINK BEST BUT REMEMBER TWO ELEMENTS
CHANCE OF WEATHER SOUTH PLUS SIGNIFICANT TIME SAVING
HELPS MAKE UP PAST DELAYS LOVE

RUSS

RUSSELL MOCK

**TELEGRAM FROM RUSS TO JERRIE IN BANGKOK, URGING HER
TO HURRY TO FINISH AHEAD OF JOAN MERRIAM SMITH**

Susan Reid collection

Once in the air, Jerrie crossed into East Pakistan, leaving behind a view of **rice paddies**. She flew over a leafy jungle canopy, and on to the Bay of Bengal, known for its fierce weather. But the day was calm, with blue skies and puffy clouds. After flying over mile after mile of jungles, Bangkok finally came into sight. As she set Charlie's wheels onto the **tarmac** of the Don Mueang International Airport, she realized the farther south she flew, the more oppressive the heat became. Once again, she arrived drenched in sweat, and with a mighty thirst. All she could think of was soaking in a cool tub of water. Jerrie could hardly hide her disappointment when she learned that Bangkok's water supply was turned off during shortages and this happened to be one of those times!

Jerrie finally broke away from customs, fees, and paperwork by late afternoon. Before leaving the airport, she had the airplane refueled. An English-speaking couple, Mr. and Mrs. Bundit Watanasupt, introduced themselves and offered to take her around Bangkok. They took her to the beautiful parks and the bustling city. She had hoped to see the Buddhist temples of Old Siam, but the attraction was shut down for the night. The Watanasupts treated Jerrie to dinner. Jerrie was thankful that she had learned to eat with chopsticks before leaving Ohio. They ate exotic dishes such as shark's fin soup and abalone stew. It was one of the most interesting and delicious meals she had ever eaten.

After dinner, she returned to the Plaza Hotel to a room with a faulty air-conditioning system. She had difficulty sleeping in the muggy room. She awoke to a loud banging on the door at 3:30 in the morning. She wished the noise would stop, but then she remembered that she had requested an early wake-up call due to the 1,300-mile flight ahead of her. The best and most direct route to the Philippines took her south of Cambodia, east towards Saigon, then across the South China Sea. After a weather briefing, she went through customs and immigration, and took off for Manila by eight o'clock, leaving the Don Mueang Airport behind. She flew past Cambodia and over Vietnam. She knew that down below a war raged, but from the skies above the jungle canopy, all looked quiet and undisturbed.

Jerrie took out a food bar and had a sip of water. She wished she could have had the long-distance radio repaired before journeying across nine hundred miles of the South China Sea. She watched cloud formations as she flew, becoming so familiar with all their variations that she could now predict headwinds and other weather conditions. She decided to take the time to write some letters, but stopped when she heard a strange noise. *Charlie's* motor no longer purred. It sounded rough. Could sand from the storm have found its way into the engine? Sweat beaded up on her forehead as she pulled on the carburetor heat to allow more air into the engine. With the increase of airflow, the engine smoothed out. *Charlie* ran better for a few hours, but with the carburetor heat on, the engine used more gas. The strong headwinds also made the gas consumption greater than she had figured. Jerrie made some mathematical calculations and discovered that she would run out of fuel unless she transferred the fuel in the cabin tank to the right wing tank. Relocating fuel midair was risky. The interruption of gas could stall the plane, and the last thing she wanted was to stall while flying over the South China Sea.

Jerrie's hands shook as she turned on the transfer pumps, letting the gas flow from the cabin tanks to the right wing tank. She wiped the sweat from her brow. *Charlie*'s engine sputtered, then it purred, but then it sputtered again. The plane hesitated. *Charlie*'s nose dropped. Without the sound of an engine, all went silent except for the beating of Jerrie's heart. It thumped in her chest as she took a deep breath, waiting for the gas to flow to the wing. Finally, the transfer was complete. She turned off the pump. *Charlie*'s engine hummed once again, along with the beating of Jerrie's heart.

With the crisis over, Jerrie took a deep breath and plopped down on the pillow, utterly exhausted. It had been ten hours since she left India. She looked out into the darkness. There was not a star in the sky, and no sign of the moon. Jerrie prayed, over and over again. Thirsty, but nearly out of water, she worried about drinking what she had, in case she found herself in a life raft drifting for days. She heard a faint noise over the short-range radio, and, less than an hour later, she was finally over land. Soon she would be in Manila.

Greeted by clapping and cheers, Jerrie got out of her plane. Many in the crowd had speculated that her flight over the ocean had ended in disaster since her landing was so far behind schedule. She posed for photos and signed autographs. Reporters and journalists came around and asked her lots and lots of questions.

"Mrs. Mock, what do you think happened to Amelia Earhart?

"Mrs. Mock, do you think you will disappear in the ocean the same way Amelia Earhart did?"

"But Mrs. Mock, your plane is so small. Smaller than Miss Earhart's."[3]

Jerrie did not want to even think about the disappearance of Amelia Earhart or her recent fear over the dark ocean waters. Despite her

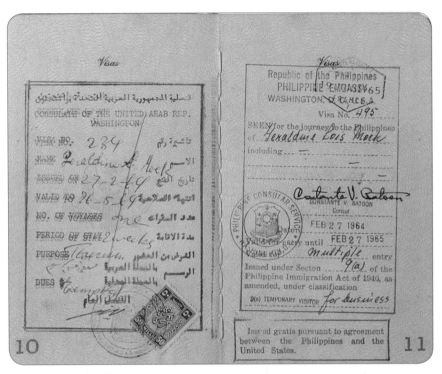

JERRIE'S PASSPORT WITH VISA STAMPS FROM THE UNITED ARAB REPUBLIC AND THE PHILIPPINES

Susan Reid collection

troubles, she had total confidence in *Charlie,* and she preferred to think positively. She sat down with the reporters and assured them that she was not worried. She believed in her plane, and she planned to fly around the world, so that's what she was going to do.

Terry Bernadino and her father, Dr. Emiliano C. Ramirez, stopped by and introduced themselves as friends of Jerrie's sister Barbara and alumni of the Ohio State University. They offered to drive Jerrie to the hotel. The reporters ignored the interruption, followed the car to the hotel, and continued their questioning in the hotel lobby.

The next day, April 9, was a national holiday in the Philippines: Bataan Day. There was a Cessna service shop in Manila, but it would be

JERRIE ENJOYS THE HOLIDAY OF BATAAN DAY IN THE COUNTRY-
SIDE OF MANILA

Courtesy of Phoenix Graphix

closed all day. Jerrie was told the parts she needed had arrived, but she would have to wait until the following morning for the long-distance radio and the brakes to be repaired. Jerrie realized there was nothing she could do to change things so she went to a beauty shop and enjoyed a lakeside lunch in a lovely lodge in the mountains.

The following day she ate at a country club while watching golfers through a window. It felt very much like home. After lunch, she checked on *Charlie*. All the repairs had been made, but her belongings were scattered all over the ground. Jerrie began the daunting task of squeezing

Thanks for all
you did to make
me beautiful
Jerrie Mock

JERRIE RELAXES IN A BEAUTY PARLOR IN MANILA

Courtesy of Phoenix Graphix

maps, spare parts, emergency equipment, and the rest of her supplies back into the tiny plane. With half of her belongings still on the ground, Jerrie was told that Russ was on the phone. She stopped what she was doing, and answered the call. Russ was upset she was still in Manila and he insisted that she needed to leave immediately. Jerrie tried to explain about the holiday, *Charlie*'s repairs, and her total exhaustion. Russ kept insisting that she leave since Joan could still beat her. As they continued to argue, the operator came on and the connection went bad. Jerrie slammed down the receiver. "I wished I couldn't hear him. What a stupid conversation. I stamped my foot at the phone, the operator, and Russ. Oh, well, even if he could hear me, it probably wouldn't matter. He just wanted a 'first.' Not me."[4]

> *Western Union Telegram*
> *April 11, 1964*
>   —*Apparently you couldn't hear. Hope you still plan to depart immediately or during the day. Smith in Bangkok. Described direct Lubon Guam to pick up time. You can win if you don't spend two days anywhere. Can you take it only day and a half in Honolulu. Don't forget you need 2,500 miles stateside. She doesn't. Russ*[5]

DID YOU KNOW?

A sari is made of silk or cotton and is draped around the waist and over one shoulder. In the Hindu tradition, girls begin to wear saris at age twelve, and continue to wear them for the rest of their lives. The men wear dhotis, a white cloth draped around their waists and legs.

GUAM, WAKE ISLAND, AND HAWAII

A T 3:30 a.m. Jerrie Mock rubbed her eyes and tried to focus on the job ahead of her. Even though she felt weary from waking at such an early hour, she prepared to travel to the island of Guam. Jerrie trudged down to the car and slept almost all the way to the airport. It was still dark when she arrived. She picked up her weather folder and her flight plan, and went to the Cessna shop to get *Charlie*. Jerrie needed to wait for the customs and immigration men before she could leave the country. The sun was coming up, and her impatience grew as she waited and waited to be cleared for takeoff. She walked out of the shop and paced beside *Charlie*. Reporters found her pacing, and they bombarded her with questions, the same old questions about Amelia Earhart. Exhausted and irritated, she felt like yelling at them. Instead, she walked back into the Cessna shop to get away from their annoying questions. Finally the airport men showed up with the necessary paperwork. Forms were signed; photos were taken. Jerrie said her good-byes and climbed aboard her plane.

Charlie's engine purred as it taxied down the runway with its new sand-free air filter. The airplane also sported new brakes, and a new motor for the long-distance radio. Jerrie smiled, excited at the thought of heading back to America, back to her family. Although Russ made her angry sometimes, she still missed him and the kids terribly. Her tiny plane lifted off the ground, up through the clouds, and past the golden sun. Jerrie marveled at "the phenomenal beauty that is God's gift, each dawn, to pilots who venture eastward over oceans."[1]

Beneath puffy clouds, Jerrie flew over endless whitecaps in the ocean below. She felt admiration for Ferdinand Magellan as she crossed the Pacific. He had sailed across this ocean in 1521. By the time his crew had sighted land and arrived in Guam, they were nearly starved to death. Hundreds of years later, Jerrie was flying over the same ocean, heading for the same island. She too felt like an explorer, journeying into the unknown, over the expansive ocean waters.

Eleven and a half hours later, *Charlie*'s wheels finally touched the ground at the Agaña Naval Air Station. Jerrie got out of the plane. Someone from the crowd shouted, "Welcome back to the United States!" Generals and admirals from the United States Air Force and Navy came to greet her, along with the governor of Guam. A United States Navy band played patriotic songs. Jerrie smiled, happy to feel so at home, even though her real home was still thousands of miles away.

Jerrie attended a reception in her honor at the airport, and was invited by Governor Guerrero and his wife to stay at their mansion. They had hoped she could stay for a couple of days, but a report came in concerning Joan Merriam Smith. Joan was leaving Calcutta and headed for Thailand. She was only a couple of days behind Jerrie, and closing in. Russell Mock called and reminded Jerrie that she needed to press on if she wanted to ensure her place in the history books. After the long, lonely flight, Jerrie wanted nothing more than to rest, to swim, and to spend more time with all the wonderful people she had just met, but she knew in her heart she needed to keep moving. She freshened up, then gave a television interview. After an enjoyable dinner with the

GUAM

GUAM IS an island in the western Pacific Ocean, and a territory of the United States of America. It is thirty miles long, and four to twelve miles wide. Ferdinand Magellan was the first European to discover the island during a Spanish Expedition on March 6, 1521. Guam was controlled by Spain until 1898, when it was surrendered to the United States during the Spanish-American War. During World War II, the Japanese captured the island soon after the bombing of Pearl Harbor. They occupied Guam until the United States fought to take it back near the end of the war. The Japanese held thousands captive at the Manenggon concentration camp, and brutal massacres were committed against the Chamorro, the people of the island. On July 21, 1944, a date now celebrated annually as Liberation Day, Guam was once again a territory of the United States of America and the people were freed. "Many of the survivors have forgiven, but they've not forgotten," Angel Sablan, director of the Mayors Council of Guam says. "The Chamorro are loving, for-giving people. . . . It's no lon-ger a time to remember what happened then, it's time to remember we are free now and we can look at our children and see smiles on their faces."[2]

GUAM

Courtesy of mapsof.net

Guerrero family, she slept for four hours before receiving her 3:30 a.m. wake-up call.

Before the break of dawn, *Charlie* raced down the runway and climbed back up in the air to begin the day trip to Wake Island. Jerrie reached her cruising altitude, leveled the plane, and set it on autopilot. After tidying up the plane, she sat back and enjoyed a breakfast bar and a drink of water. Then she got out her stationery and wrote letters to her family. In between writing, she watched the cloud formations and tried to avoid headwinds. The rain fell, forming rainbows below the clouds. Jerrie flew above the clouds and missed the showers, but the turbulence was so rough she banged her head. She quickly put her pen away and quit writing. The rough skies served as a reminder that many considered the trip to Wake Island the most dangerous leg of her flight around the world. There were no beacons in the ocean. She had to rely on her long-distance radio to guide her, with outbound beams from Guam, and inbound beams from Wake Island. Since Wake Island is only fifteen miles in diameter, flying just one degree off course would make her miss the island by thirty miles. Precision was everything.

While she flew over the ocean, pilots talked to her over the radio. One pilot seemed amazed that she flew in a single-engine plane. He had said, "I wouldn't fly across the bay in a little thing like that."[3] But Jerrie loved her little plane and wouldn't have wanted to be in any other. She and *Charlie* were a team. She settled in for the long flight and found comfort in the sound of a beacon beeping from Wake Island. In the darkened skies, lights shone in the distance. Suddenly, a cloud engulfed her plane and she couldn't see a thing. She called to the control tower, but she didn't understand what they were saying. She dropped the plane below the clouds, and the runway lights at the airport shone like stars. A person in the control tower came back on the radio. She followed his instructions and turned for the runway, but the sky "seemed to explode with white fire."[4] Jerrie jumped at the sight. Was someone shooting at her? She knew she had obtained all the permissions to land. Why would anyone be shooting her out of the sky?

She landed with a thud, happy to be out of the air and safe on the ground. Hundreds of people gathered around as she climbed out of her plane. She recalls, "A lei of seashells was thrown about my neck. I was kissed, 'Aloha.' Almost everyone took pictures and all the young-sters wanted autographs. I was overwhelmed."[5]

Hal Sellers of the Federal Aviation Administration assured Jerrie that no one had been shooting at her. A flare was launched to help her locate the airport amid the thick cloud cover. He offered Jerrie some food, and took her to a home in an FAA housing complex along the ocean. Soon she was fast asleep, lulled by the rhythmic pounding of the surf. The next morning, she awoke to the sound of the waves crashing against the shoreline. She pulled on a pair of slacks, and rushed out to see the island without even putting on her lipstick.

Jerrie marveled at the sight of white sand surrounded by clear blue water. Huge waves beat against the coral reef and sprayed her. She looked across the road and noticed that seaplanes had landed overnight in the turquoise lagoon. Jerrie crossed the white coral road, sat down on a rock, and let the cool waters splash her feet. After enjoying the peaceful scenery, she went back inside and did some laundry.

Hal Sellers picked Jerrie up and drove her to the airport to take care of her preflight needs. The weatherman at the airport suggested delaying her departure for Hawaii due to a squall line. He explained that if she left in the afternoon, she would be sure to run into a storm in the middle of the night. He advised her to leave that night, so she would hit the bad weather at dawn, when she could see to fly around it. Jerrie decided to take his advice and leave that evening, with hopes that she would have time to swim in the Pacific Ocean during the day. After getting her paperwork in order, she went to a luncheon party at the Wake Island Bowling Center. It was a fancy affair complete with china, sparkling glassware, and white linen tablecloths. After lunch, she went sightseeing around the island.

After touring the island, Jerrie swam in a swimming hole in a shel-tered lagoon, so there would be no chance of swimming with sharks.

WAKE ISLAND ALBATROSSES

WAKE ISLAND is a bird sanctuary, and thousands of albatrosses, otherwise known as gooney birds, spend their winters on the island. When Jerrie was driving on the island, the birds had not yet left for their summer home, and were so plentiful that her car windows needed to be closed to keep them out. Fearlessly, the gooney birds landed on the hood and the top of the car.

The birds are protected, but having so many of them in the area is a danger to airplanes, since they can be sucked into an airplane engine, causing it to stall. Jerrie couldn't believe how they tumbled and fell with nearly every landing. The sight was comical. Not only did they have rough landings, but almost every takeoff was unsuccessful. The gooney birds would try again and again until they finally were airborne. Once in the air, the birds, with wingspans of up to eleven feet, flew more gracefully than any bird she had ever seen.

A FLOCK OF ALBATROSSES, OR GOONEY BIRDS, WHICH WINTER ON WAKE ISLAND

Courtesy of Phoenix Graphix

Before she left, Jerrie hoped to have her souvenir airmail covers stamped to prove she had been on Wake Island. Airmail covers were envelopes with commemorative markings that made great souvenirs. Each envelope had an Amelia Earhart airmail stamp, and the postmark, "Columbus, Ohio, March 19, 1964." The problem was the post office closed in a half an hour. She had a thousand airmail covers, and they all needed to be addressed before the post office would cancel them with a stamp. Hal and Jerrie recruited the help of some FAA secretaries. Working as a team, they addressed envelopes, and had seven hundred covers stamped and mailed before closing time.

About 8:00 that evening, Hal took Jerrie to a bowling alley to enjoy one of the best burgers on the island. Jerrie relished this taste of home, but it made her more than a little homesick. She missed her family terribly and wondered what they were doing. She couldn't wait to see her boys and hug her little girl again. Before she and Hal left for the airport, the manager of the bowling alley came out with a care package consisting of a roast veal sandwich and an orange. Jerrie didn't have much of an appetite. She kindly explained to the thoughtful man that she didn't have room in her plane for such a big box of food, and she was afraid such a large sandwich might go to waste. The man seemed disappointed, but he put some of the food into a smaller box and Jerrie went on her way to Honolulu.

Charlie's wheels raced down the runway at 10:30 p.m. Soon the little plane was up in the air above the rolling ocean waves. The long-distance radio was quiet. The darkness and the hum of the plane's engine made Jerrie's eyes feel heavy. She was alone in the black night, but she was not lonely. She was thrilled to be flying over the ocean, with *Charlie* as her only companion. Seven hours later, when dawn broke, she welcomed the sight of the bright sunshine. Water streamed from the bottom of the clouds, and with the help of the sun, beautiful rainbows formed.

Jerrie remembers, "That day I felt like a queen, or at least a fairy princess, monarch of all I surveyed. My subjects, the foamy clouds and glowing rainbows, put on a command performance just for me. It was worth all the hard work, worry, and the past few sleepless nights. After Christopher Columbus discovered America, he became the Admiral of the Ocean Seas. In my red-and-white *Spirit of Columbus,* for a few days I became the Queen of the Ocean Skies."[6]

The weather report had promised tailwinds to push her along in her upcoming flight, but Jerrie fought headwinds the entire trip to Honolulu. After spending nearly sixteen hours in the air, Jerrie had been awake for a full thirty hours. She approached the airport twelve miles south of course. Because of the clouds and mountains in the area, the air traffic controller recommended a radar landing, allowing them to direct her to the correct runway with the use of radar. Jerrie was worn out! She agreed, and after a smooth landing, she taxied to the terminal.

A large crowd pushed up against the chain-link fence. When *Charlie* came to a stop, hundreds of people swarmed around the little plane. Jerrie stepped out and the immigration man looked over her paperwork. As soon as he was finished, leis of red and white flowers were put around Jerrie's neck. The crowd shouted, "Aloha!"

Jerrie was handed a telephone, and was surprised to hear the voice of her husband. She was annoyed at his ability to track her down, but, as all eyes were upon her, she smiled. Russ told her he had canceled all

ALOHA

THE WORD *Aloha* has a much deeper meaning than just hello or good-bye. It describes an attitude or "way of life," a code of ethics taught to children. The code is derived from one of the acronyms of Aloha.

A-ala, watchful, alertness
L-lokahi, working with unity
O-oia'l'o, truthful honesty
H-ha'aha'a, humility
A-ahonui, patient perseverance[7]

the receptions and parties that had been planned in her honor since he felt that she needed to get her rest more than anything else. Although his intentions were good, Jerrie was furious! She felt heat rise to her face. How could he do this to her? She never slept during the day. How could she sleep when there was a beautiful island to explore and so many wonderful people to meet? She told Russ, "But I'm not tired. Not now that I'm here. How could you ruin things before I even got here?"[8] She hung up the phone. Although surrounded by beautiful scenery and friendly people, she felt all alone. There would be no parties. All the festivities had been canceled.

Jerrie was driven to a hotel and checked into a room with a balcony that overlooked a garden of flowers. Everyone kept telling her that no one would bother her, that she would be left alone. Not even phone calls would be allowed through. No one seemed to understand that she had been alone long enough. The requests they were following came from Russ, not her. But the decisions had been made and no one would listen to her.

The sound of waves crashing onto the beach mingling with a melody and singing voices caught Jerrie's attention. She stepped out onto the balcony of her room. It overlooked a garden of exotic flowers; their fragrance drifted up to the balcony. Two women stood among the flowers singing island songs while one of them played the guitar. The smell of the flowers and the sound of the beautiful voices enchanted Jerrie. Too excited to sleep, she left her room to explore the island on her own. After wandering aimlessly for hours in search of a beach, she gave up. Sightseeing without an escort proved pointless. Jerrie returned to her hotel and stopped at the restaurant for a meal of coconut chicken. The waiter frowned and glared as he served her. In 1964, it wasn't considered appropriate for ladies to dine alone, and her waiter made sure to show his displeasure. Jerrie paid her bill, returned to her room, and was finally lulled to sleep by the sound of island music.

The next morning Jerrie arose early and headed for the airport. She wished she could explore all of the Hawaiian Islands in her small plane, but she needed to keep one step ahead of Joan Merriam Smith.

IN HONOLULU, JERRIE'S SMILE TURNS INTO A FROWN AS SHE
LEARNS THAT RUSS HAS CANCELED ALL PARTIES AND CELEBRA-
TIONS IN HER HONOR SO SHE COULD GET SOME REST

Courtesy of Phoenix Graphix

Joan had left Thailand and was in Singapore. Jerrie's next stop was Oakland, on the United States mainland. Before departing, Jerrie called Russ to give him material for a news story. While she had him on the phone, Jerrie explained that she wasn't being irresponsible and just having fun. She knew people were counting on her, and she didn't want to let them down. But she also didn't want to rush things to the point it could become dangerous, even life-threatening. With all their mis-communications out of the way, Russ promised to meet her at the air-port in California. After the phone call, she went to get her plane ready for her longest flight yet—over seventeen hours from Honolulu to Oakland. Jerrie Mock left behind the white sandy beaches, turquoise waters, and swaying palm trees of Hawaii, and pointed *Charlie*'s nose to the east, toward home.

DID YOU KNOW?

A legendary shark swims around Wake Island. His name is Mag-Check Charlie. He is a smart shark with good ears, who swims around the island, living off the remains of unlucky aviators. When a pilot takes his plane to the end of the run-way to check the engine magnetos before takeoff, legend says that Mag-Check Charlie listens very carefully to see if the engine sounds rough. If he detects a rough magneto or other unusual sounds, he swims to the far end of the runway, wait-ing for his dinner.

HOME!

JERRIE FLEW most of the day, but she still needed to fly through the night. In order to prepare for an all-night flight, Jerrie had practiced staying awake all evening in a chair at home, but it never worked. She couldn't reproduce the element of danger in her living room, and she always fell sound asleep. Now, as she flew over the whitecaps of the endless ocean, sleeping was not an option. She placed a mask over her nose and mouth to breathe in pure oxygen for ten minutes every hour. She also concentrated on the sound of the steady signal of the Conso-lan station. Thoughts of going home to see Russ and the kids kept her awake and excited, but she felt a little sadness on ending her adventure around the world.

Thirty-eight **nautical miles** from the airport in California, Jerrie looked down at the Farrallon Islands, her first sight of land. Soon after, the Oakland International Airport came into view. Thrilled to be back in the States, she landed the plane hard and fast. *Charlie* hit the airstrip with a thud, and the little plane bounced down the runway. Jerrie felt a little embarrassed at such a rough landing in front of the large crowd, but her happy mood kept her from thinking about it for very long. As she rolled to the terminal, an enormous throng of people rushed to the plane. They shouted and waved their arms. She tried not to hit the hundreds of well-wishers swarming about *Charlie*. Her airplane rolled to a stop and Jerrie shut off the engine. Someone opened *Charlie*'s door. After so many hours of silence, the noise of the outside world came crashing in.

Russ pushed his way through the crowd, climbed up on the Cessna's step, and gave his wife many "welcome home" kisses. Jerrie held her skirt down as she stepped from the plane. She accepted a large bouquet of flowers while struggling to put on her high heels and comb her hair. People pushed and shoved, trying to shake her hand and welcome her home. Torally exhausted, Jerrie needed to get away from the throngs of well-wishers and get some much needed rest.

Russ led her into a lounge, but some reporters and cameramen followed. When Jerrie finished posing for photos, Russ introduced her to Darlene Ceremello, a shy girl about nineteen years old. She was about to enter a convent and, as part of her vows, needed to give away everything she owned. The young girl explained that she had been praying for Mrs. Mock's safety. She handed Jerrie her gold Saint Christopher's medal. Jerrie happily accepted the gift. She added it to her charm bracelet and promised to wear it every day. "After flying the Pacific alone, with only God to protect me, I realize the power of His grace. I was grateful for the prayers of this girl, and of all of the other people who had prayed for my safety."[1]

Jerrie made the preflight arrangements for the following day and left with Russ to get some rest at a nearby hotel. She opened the door to a room filled with flowers, telegrams, fruit baskets, and a bottle of champagne. Jerrie made a call to Newark, Ohio, to speak with her mom and dad and assure them that she was safely in the United States. Russ told her how much the boys had missed her and how excited they were that she was almost home. Valerie sent a special message, "Tell Mommy

RUSSELL GREETS JERRIE WITH A BOUQUET OF FLOWERS AT THE
OAKLAND INTERNATIONAL AIRPORT IN CALIFORNIA

Reprinted with permission from the *Columbus Dispatch*

I love her lots, as much as the whole world, the ocean, and the sky."[2] Jerrie smiled at the thought of holding her little girl in her arms again.

After a nice dinner and a good night's sleep, Jerrie was off to the airport for the final stage of her quest to fly around the world. She lightened her load by removing the life raft and some overseas charts and maps since she no longer needed to fly over the vast oceans. Now she would be flying over the mountains, valleys, rivers, and lakes of the United States of America. Homesick for her children, she couldn't wait to get across the country. She ached to be with them and wished she could fly straight home, straight into their arms. But that was not an option. In order to meet the 22,858 **statute miles** (the distance around the world at the Tropic of Cancer) required by the Fédération Aéronautique Internationale she needed to add some distance to the trip for an official circling of the earth.

After almost twenty-four hours, on the morning of April 16, she left California. She led the press to believe she was headed for Phoenix, when in reality her plan was to make a short five-and-a-half-hour flight to Tucson, Arizona. She didn't feel comfortable with all the fanfare and wanted to be alone in her plane. She could finally relax a little because Joan Merriam Smith was still in Indonesia, with five more stops to make before completing her trip in California.

In Tucson, one reporter showed up and asked Jerrie some questions. He wrote an article saying that the record-breaking pilot seemed to be hiding from the press. After spending the night at the airport hotel, she flew 267 miles to El Paso, Texas. A large group had assembled to meet and greet her. There were lots of lady flyers, including Ruth Deerman, the president of the Ninety-Nines. An international organization of woman pilots, the Ninety-Nines was founded in 1929 with ninety-nine women pilots. Their first president was Amelia Earhart. The group had planned a party for Jerrie, but she was unable to stay. A storm was moving across the path she planned to take to reach Columbus. She needed to get back up in the air immediately, or she could be stuck for days. Jerrie felt awful to have to disappoint so many people who had worked hard in her honor, but she had no choice. She quickly waved good-bye to all her fans and fellow pilots, and flew up into the dark rainy skies.

The front was moving fast, headed for Memphis, and so was Jerrie. Bolts of lightning flashed in the darkened sky. Jerrie pushed her little plane a little faster and prayed. "And God must have heard, because miraculously, we always found a place to slide through. It was good to know I wasn't up there alone."[3] Because of the bad weather, she was forced to fly at a lower altitude. She had hoped to make it all the way to Columbus nonstop, but the lower altitude and the faster speeds made the engine use more fuel. Jerrie looked at her gauges. She didn't want to end her around-the-world adventure with an emergency landing in a cornfield, so she touched down in Bowling Green, Kentucky, to get a quick splash of fuel.

Back in the air, during the final hop of her around-the-world adventure, feelings of excitement were shadowed by melancholy thoughts. "I had come to think of the little Cessna as something more than an engineering design translated into nuts and bolts and airfoils. It seemed almost alive—a real friend. *Charlie* seemed to enjoy the oceans and deserts as much as I, except when he got sand in his carburetor. I patted the top of his tan instrument panel and thanked him for taking such good care of me. And I thanked God for flying along."[4] Jerrie made her final approach to Port Columbus, called the control tower, and awaited instructions. With a huge grin she looked down at the airport, the place where it all began, hardly believing that she had actually finished what she had started out to do twenty-nine days ago.

Jerrie's nerves tingled. She was home! Finally home! A crowd of five thousand had assembled at Port Columbus, waiting since 6:00 p.m. The loud drone of *Charlie's* engine could be heard around 9:30 p.m. The air traffic controller instructed Jerrie to make a low pass down runway nine so the NAA observer could clock her for the official record. She was so excited to be reunited with her family, she nearly forgot she was setting a world record. Right at that moment, Jerrie fully realized that she had earned her place in the record books; no one could ever take that away

THOUSANDS GATHERED TO WELCOME BACK THEIR HOME-TOWN HERO

Courtesy of Phoenix Graphix

from her. Her emotions exploded with feelings of pride and humility, thankfulness and joy, all colliding together at once.

Jerrie dropped *Charlie* down and revved the engine, letting the little plane roar as it zoomed past the crowd. Then she turned *Charlie* back around and made her final approach to runway thirty. Once the wheels touched the ground, the tower controller told her to come to a stop so they could push *Charlie* the rest of the way to the terminal. Jerrie saw the huge crowd that had gathered and she understood that they were trying to keep everyone safe.

People pushed and shouted, waving their arms and holding up signs, welcoming their hometown hero. Even her childhood girlfriends from the class of '43 held up a "Welcome Home" sign. The door of her

A JUBILANT JERRIE LANDS IN COLUMBUS, OHIO, THE FIRST
WOMAN TO FLY SOLO AROUND THE WORLD

Courtesy of Phoenix Graphix

plane opened. Russ and their two sons, Roger and Gary, embraced her
with hugs and lots of kisses. Flashbulbs popped, and questions were fired
at her. The one face Jerrie wanted to see most of all was that of her little
girl. Russ found Valerie and handed the terrified toddler to her mother.
Realizing that Valerie was afraid of the noisy crowd, Jerrie held her tight
as she stepped down from the plane.

Governor James A. Rhodes placed an enormous lei of orchids
around her neck, and she was whisked to a special platform. Her mom
and dad, her sisters, Barbara and Susan, and her grandfather, Raymond
Wright, all gathered around her. Mel Tharp from the *Columbus Evening
Dispatch* presented a golden necklace with a globe-shaped pendant. A
ruby marked every place she had landed, and a diamond represented
Columbus, Ohio. Mayor Sensenbrenner and other politicians welcomed
her home. General Lassiter smiled at Jerrie and said, "Two years ago,
when you first started talking about this, I had a lot of skepticism."

FOUR OF JERRIE'S NEWARK HIGH SCHOOL CLASSMATES GREET HER UPON HER RETURN. *LEFT TO RIGHT:* MRS. WILLIAM T. (MIXIE) HECKELMAN, MRS. GEORGE B. (RITA) BECKMAN, MRS. RICHARD (LOIS) DUNN, AND MRS. THOMAS (GINNY) WEISS

Reprinted with permission from the *Columbus Dispatch*

She smiled up at him, and said, "I know!"[5]

Jerrie was overwhelmed by all the attention she received from the thousands of people in the crowd. They all wanted to shake her hand, get autographs, and take photos with her. She said, "It didn't seem right that these people should say such wonderful things about me; I just had fun flying my airplane."[6]

After a lifetime of dreams and years of preparation, Jerrie Mock had achieved her goal of flying in her plane and seeing the world. "You

JERRIE (*CENTER*) POSES AT HOME WITH (*LEFT TO RIGHT*) GRAND-
FATHER RAYMOND HARLEY WRIGHT, MOTHER BLANCHE,
DAUGHTER VALERIE, AND SISTERS BARBARA AND SUSAN

Susan Reid collection

know," Jerrie said, "even when I left Columbus, I think a lot of people
were skeptical about what I planned—they thought maybe I would get
to Bermuda, maybe get stuck some place farther on. What seemed to
impress everyone most was that I did it in a single-engine plane."[7] But
Jerrie had believed in her dream, and she understood that you had to
have a dream to make a dream come true. And after twenty-nine days,
twenty-one takeoffs and landings, and 22,860 miles, she became the first
woman to fly around the world—solo!

WHERE IS JOAN?

AFTER JERRIE MOCK had completed her solo trip around the world and earned her place in the history books, Joan Merriam Smith still needed to travel from Lae, Papua New Guinea, to Guam, to Wake Island, to Honolulu, and, finally, back to where her flight began, Oakland, California. Joan completed her around-the-world flight on May 12, 1964, twenty-five days after Jerrie landed in Columbus, Ohio.

DID YOU KNOW?

In 1942 World War I flying ace Eddie Rickenbacker crashed his plane in the South Pacific while on a special assignment for Secretary of War Henry Stimson. He and his crew had floated on a raft for twenty-four days before being rescued.[8] Jerrie Mock attracted the largest crowd to the Oakland International Airport since Eddie Rickenbacker did on his return to the United States.

FLIGHT TWELVE

SUPERSONIC JETS AND RECORD-BREAKING STREAKS

Ｎｅｗｓ ｏｆ Jerrie's accomplishment seemed to travel at the speed of light. When she landed in Columbus, Joan Merriam Smith was in Australia, about to leave for Lae, Papua New Guinea, the island Amelia Earhart took off from before her disappearance. Joan sent a telegram that said, "Sincere congratulations on your great achievement. Hoping the clear skies and tailwinds of your trip will always be with you."[1] Muriel Earhart Morrissey, the sister of Amelia Earhart, wrote, "I rejoice with you as you complete your successful flight. I am sure Amelia's courageous spirit rode with you all the way."[2] Jerrie especially treasured the note from Amelia's sister, since Amelia's air travels had inspired Jerrie to see the world.

When Jerrie first returned home, she had a hard time getting back into her routine as a housewife. Her list was long: doing laundry, shopping for groceries, cleaning house, and caring for the kids. She even had plans for a trip to the beauty parlor. But neighbors popped in, hoping for autographs and photos with their hometown hero. The phone kept ringing. Townspeople planned a day full of festivities followed by a concert performed by the Newark High School band. The first time Jerrie tried to prepare dinner for her family proved overwhelming. The local newspaper reported, "She'll be back on full-time duty in the kitchen beginning Sunday when her mother-in-law goes home to Bridgeport, Conn. It'll probably be a long time before she can put on an apron and spend several hours in the kitchen."[3]

At the end of the flight, Jerrie never flew *Charlie* again. The plane was retired, and the Cessna Company presented Jerrie with a brand new Cessna 206, which she named *Mike*. At first, *Charlie* went to the Javelin Aircraft Company owned by Dave Blanton. Then the record-breaking airplane went on display at the Cessna factory in Wichita, Kansas. Today, *Charlie* hangs at the National Air and Space Museum Steven F. Udvar-Hazy Center in Virginia.

A few weeks after Jerrie's historic flight, she and her family were invited to the White House. She nearly declined the invitation since May 4 was her daughter Valerie's fourth birthday, but President Lyndon B. Johnson promised a birthday party for Valerie in the Rose Garden. President Johnson lit the candles on the chocolate-frosted birthday cake, and little Valerie blew them out. Valerie shyly thanked the president, but she turned her face away when he tried to give her a kiss.

Following the birthday celebration, the attention turned from Valerie to her mom. President Johnson placed an orange ribbon attached to a ten-karat gold medal around Jerrie Mock's neck, and presented her with the Federal Aviation Agency's Gold Medal of Exceptional Service. He said, "Your tremendous solo exploit in **circumnavigating** the globe in a light plane adds another notation to the record book of American triumphs, one already replete with the aeronautical exploits of American women. This latest feat fills every American with pride. On behalf of the nation, I extend my congratulations."[4]

After her record-breaking flight, Jerrie gave many talks, accepted numerous awards, and set more records. In 1965, she rode shotgun in the pace car at the Indianapolis 500. She appeared on the hit television

To Jerrie Mock —
whose hand has rocked the cradle
and girdled the globe.

Lyndon B Johnson

AT THE WHITE HOUSE, JERRIE ACCEPTS A MEDAL FROM PRESI-
DENT LYNDON B. JOHNSON IN THE ROSE GARDEN ON MAY 4,
1964. SHE RECEIVED THE HIGHEST AVIATION AWARD, THE FED-
ERAL AVIATION AGENCY'S DECORATION FOR EXCEPTIONAL
SERVICE

U.S. government photo

program, *To Tell the Truth*. The popular talk show, *The Mike Douglas Show,* invited Jerrie as a guest. She was given the keys to ten cities and was granted eighteen honorary memberships, including one to the 87th Fighter Interceptor Squadron of the United States Air Force. She was inducted into the Ohio Women's Hall of Fame in 1979, the Licking County Hall of Fame in 1981, and the City of Columbus Hall of Fame in October 2014.

After all her numerous appearances and many speeches, Jerrie Mock longed to be back in a plane, where she felt the most at home. She had earned celebrity status, but she preferred to be alone in her plane, not attending so many functions. She wondered what all the fuss was about. "Planes are made to be flown," she had said. "I was just out having a little fun in my plane."[5]

In July 1964, Jerrie was invited by the United States Air Force to fly in a F-101 Voodoo fighter jet. Sporting an orange flight suit, a helmet, and an oxygen mask over her nose and mouth, she was hitched to

a parachute and boarded the rear of the cockpit of a needle-nosed jet. Captain Eugene L. Weidel of the 87th Fighter Interceptor Squadron at Lockbourne Air Force Base manned the controls. The **afterburners** kicked in when the twin jet took off, pushing Jerrie Mock back in her seat. They traveled faster than the speed of sound, a sizzling 1,038 miles per hour, as opposed to *Charlie*'s cruising speed of 155 miles per hour. The trip—from Columbus, Ohio, to Toledo, on to Cleveland, then back to Columbus—took less than one hour. "Fantastic," was how she described it to a reporter. "It was just fantastic. It was the most thrilling thing I've ever done." At one point Captain Weidel had Jerrie take over the controls. "It was a wonderful flight," she said. "I didn't want to come down."[6]

Of course, she finally did have to come down, but not for long. In 1966, Jerrie set a woman's speed record over a 312-mile **closed course**, flying an Aero Commander 200 at speeds of 206.7 miles per hour. In

JERRIE CLIMBS ABOARD AN AIR FORCE F-101 VOODOO FIGHTER
SUPERSONIC JET

U.S. government photo

1966, the space race had everyone's attention. Who would get to the moon first, Russia or the United States? Jerrie Mock claims if she had been younger when she returned from her flight around the world, she would have flown to the moon.[7] Although she didn't have a rocket ship, she did have a little plane and a big heart. When she learned that three Russian women had taken the international record for straight-line distance from her hero Amelia Earhart, she set out to beat the Russians at what she did best—flying. The record set by Marina Raskova, Polina Osipenko, and Valentina Grizodubova on September 24–25, 1938, earned them Hero of the Soviet Union titles from Joseph Stalin. They flew their Tupolev ANT-37 long-range bomber, named *Rodina,* 3,672 miles in twenty-six hours and twenty-nine minutes.[8]

Jerrie crushed the Russian record on April 9–10, 1966, flying 4,528 miles from Honolulu to Columbus, bringing the international record for straight-line distance for a woman back to the United States of America. She landed at Port Columbus after thirty-one hours in the air, nonstop. Ohio Governor James A. Rhodes was at the airport to greet her, along with a large crowd of proud Americans. On April 15, Governor Rhodes sent a congratulatory letter to Jerrie naming her "Ambassador of the Airways." A couple of years later, on June 28–29, 1968, she shattered another world speed record for women, flying from Columbus to Puerto Rico and back in thirty-three hours without stopping. Jerrie had said, "Columbus is an air-minded city, and I really hope what I've accomplished will help aviation."[9]

Keeping up with all the expenses to own and fly her new Cessna became difficult. There were sponsors to pay back and bills that had piled up. With a compassionate heart for the needy, Jerrie decided to donate her airplane, *Mike,* to a good cause. In 1969, she gave her Cessna 206 to Father Anthony Gendusa, for use on his rounds of mercy missions in Lae, Papua New Guinea. While flying to the small island off the coast of Australia, Jerrie broke nine world speed records. After she landed, Jerrie stayed for a month doing missionary work with Father Gendusa. They visited leper colonies and worked with underprivileged

Carried aboard speed record flight, on Aero Commander 200, September 28, 1966

N260M

500-kilometer closed course speed record for class Clb. Columbus, O./Henderson OMNI Sta., W.Va./Bellaire OMNI Sta., O./Columbus, O. Speed: 206.7 MPH

Jerrie Mock

COLUMBUS, OHIO
SEP 28 1966 P.M.
AIRPORT MAIL FACILITY

U·S·AIR MAIL 8¢

Jerrie Mock
2490 Bexford Pl
Columbus, O

Carried aboard Cessna P-206 N155JM on straight-line distance flight, April 9-10, 1966

N155JM

Official record flight, for non-stop distance in a straight line for women. Honolulu, H.I. to Columbus, Ohio. 4,500 miles.

Jerrie Mock

AMF COLUMBUS, OHIO
AP 11 P.A
1966

VIA AIR MAIL

U·S·AIR MAIL 8¢

Jerrie Mock
2490 Bexford Pl
Columbus, O

N65

Carried by
Jerrie Mock
June 28-29, 1968

WORLD CLOSED COURSE DISTANCE RECORDS

Class C1d and Feminine
4,085 Miles . . . and
"Speed Over Recognized Courses"

Class C1d and Feminine
Columbus-San Juan, San Juan-Columbus
Columbus-San Juan-Columbus

AMF COLUMBUS
JU 24 AM
1968

50TH ANNIVERSARY U.S. AIR MAIL SERVICE
10¢

Jerrie Mock
2490 Bexford Pl
Columbus, O.

AIRMAIL CARRIER CARDS CELEBRATING JERRIE'S RECORD-BREAKING CLOSED-COURSE SPEED RECORD ON SEPTEMBER 28, 1966; HER RECORD NONSTOP FLIGHT FROM HONOLULU TO COLUMBUS, OHIO, ON APRIL 10, 1966; AND HER CLOSED-COURSE DISTANCE RECORD ON JUNE 29, 1968

Jerrie Mock collection

JERRIE WITH THE AERO COMMANDER PLANE WITH WHICH SHE
SET THE WORLD CLOSED-COURSE SPEED RECORD

Reprinted with permission from the *Columbus Dispatch*

children.[10] When she returned to the United States, the missionary group
called the Flying Padres named Jerrie Mock an honorary member for
her hard work and sacrifices.

Jerrie had a compassionate heart, but she also had a competitive
spirit. "I took or overtook twenty-one world records," she had said.[11]
According to the National Aeronautics Association, six of her records
still stood in 2014. Jerrie has had many accomplishments in her lifetime, and it all began with her world-record flight around the globe.
But Jerrie Mock never became a household name as did Amelia Earhart. Always humble, she never sought the spotlight, but only yearned
to follow her dreams.

As a little girl, Jerrie believed she could do anything she set her
mind to. When she became a young adult, she envisioned traveling
around the world. "Let's just say that along the way I became practical
and believed in the lie—that girls couldn't do things," she said. "And

JERRIE WITH AUTOGRAPH-SEEKING NEIGHBORHOOD KIDS

Reprinted with permission from the *Columbus Dispatch*

then one day I said—I'm going to do it. And I did it."[12] When asked if she had been able to see all the exotic places she had read about as a child, she just smiled and said, "I rode a camel, saw the pyramids, and had tea in a teahouse of the King of Morocco. But because the flight was a race, I couldn't stay long in any one place."[13]

Jerrie Mock passed away peacefully with loved ones by her side on September 30, 2014, in her home in Quincy, Florida. Shortly before her death, Jerrie made her final flight plan. She had asked to be flown over Ball Point State Park and Alligator Point in Florida, an area in which she had enjoyed family vacations, then have her ashes dropped from an airplane into the Gulf of Mexico. She wanted the memorial to take place on her favorite day of the year, April 17. Due to stormy weather, Jerrie's final flight was delayed until April 22, 2015. A replica of Jerrie's beloved *Charlie* escorted the aerial funeral procession.

THE UNITED STATES AIR FORCE HONORED JERRIE WITH A
STREET AT RICKENBACKER AFB, LOCKBOURNE, OHIO

Susan Reid collection

Jerrie Mock, just an ordinary person, leads us to believe that when you set your mind to it, with hard work and determination, anything is possible. She had once said, "When I was a little girl, I used to be thrilled when I'd read about things like this, not a flight specifically but something like this. Always, I had the feeling that I was supposed to do something special, that I must really. So now I have."[14]

DID YOU KNOW?

Governor James Rhodes named Jerrie "Ohio's Golden Eagle," and Mayor Jack Sensenbrenner named April 17 "Jerrie Mock Day." Jerrie preferred not to celebrate birthdays, and she never bothered to make note of her wedding anniversary, but on April 17, she happily celebrated the day her dreams came true, the day she landed at Port Columbus, and became the first woman to fly solo around the world. Happy Jerrie Mock Day!

BLUE SKIES
ALWAYS

Jerrie's Timeline

1925	*November 22:* Geraldine "Jerrie" Fredritz is born in Newark, Ohio.
1932	*Summer:* Jerrie takes her first plane ride at a local festival.
1943	*September 27:* Jerrie begins classes at the Ohio State University, Columbus, Ohio.
1945	*March 21:* Jerrie marries her high school sweetheart, Russell Charles "Russ" Mock.
1946	*November 6:* Jerrie's first child, Roger, is born.
1947	*November 8:* Jerrie's second son, Gary, is born.
1952	Russ and Jerrie purchase their first plane, a 1946 Luscombe, named *Tweety Bird.*
1954	*December 17:* Jerrie attends OSU Department of Commerce.
1956	*September:* Jerrie makes her first solo cross-country flight to Kelley's Island in Lake Erie.
1958	*Summer:* Jerrie obtains her private pilot's license.
1960	*May 4:* Jerrie's only daughter, Valerie, is born.
1961	Jerrie manages Price Field Airport. She partners with Eugene "Whitey" Jost and forms the Jost & Mock Aero Services.
1962	With a friend, Alfred J. Baumeister, Russ and Jerrie purchase a Cessna 180. That same year Jerrie contacts the NAA and learns that no woman has officially flown around the world.
1964	*January 28:* Jerrie's passport is issued.
	March 19: Jerrie begins her attempt to become the first woman to fly solo around the world.
	April 17: Jerrie lands at Port Columbus Airport as the first woman to fly solo around the world after flying twenty-nine days and 22,860 miles.
	July 15: Jerrie flies in a supersonic F-101 Voodoo jet fighter.

1966	*April 9–10:* Jerrie sets a record for nonstop straight-line flight for women: 4,528 miles.
	July 1–2: Jerrie sets a record for nonstop flight over a closed course: 3,750 miles.
	September 28: Jerrie sets a 500-kilometer closed-course speed record: 206.7 miles per hour.
1968	*June 28–29:* Jerrie sets a world closed-course record for speed over a recognized course: 4,085 miles.
1969	*October 30:* Jerrie sets nine records in eleven days as she delivers and donates her Cessna P-206 to a missionary priest in Papua New Guinea.
1970	*January 1:* Jerrie's book, *Three-Eight Charlie,* is published by Lippincott.
1979	Jerrie and Russ divorce.
1990	*November 1:* Gary Mock dies in Tallahassee, Florida.
1991	*March 8:* Russell Mock dies.
1992	*June:* Jerrie moves to Quincy, Florida.
2007	*November 22:* Roger Mock dies in Havana, Florida.
2014	*April 17:* A life-size bronze sculpture of Jerrie Mock is unveiled at Port Columbus International Airport, and Jerrie receives Congressional recognition in celebration of the fiftieth anniversary of her historic flight around the world.
	September 30: Jerrie dies in Quincy, Florida.
	October 13: Jerrie is inducted into the Columbus Hall of Fame in Columbus, Ohio.
2015	*December 17:* First Flight Society, Kitty Hawk, North Carolina, chooses Jerrie as a person outstanding in the field of aviation, nationally and internationally.

Jerrie's Achievements
& Awards

"Firsts"

First woman to fly across both the Atlantic and Pacific Oceans
First woman to fly across the Pacific Ocean from west to east
First woman to fly across the Pacific Ocean in a single-engine plane
First woman to fly across the Pacific Ocean in both directions
First woman to fly from the United States to Africa via the North Atlantic
First woman to fly solo around the world
First woman to land a plane in Saudi Arabia

Medals and Awards

Aero Classic Aviation Progress Award
Aero Club Special Award, Wadsworth, Ohio
Amelia Earhart Memorial Award
American Institute of Aeronautics and Astronautics Special Award
Citation of Wichita, Kansas, Chamber of Commerce
Columbus Area of Commerce Award of the Year
Columbus Area of Commerce Special Award for Service to the Community
Columbus, Ohio, Hall of Fame
Columbus Transportation Club Special Award
Experimental Aircraft Association Special Award
Federal Aviation Agency Gold Medal for Exceptional Service
Glenn Hammond Curtiss Silver Medal, Pittsburgh OX-5 Club
Kansas 99s Special Recognition Medallion
Licking County Historical Society, Award of Appreciation

Louis Bleriot Silver Medal

Milestones in Manned Flight Trophy, Trans World Airlines

National Aviation Trades Association Special Award

National Pilots' Association Pilot-of-the Year Award

Newark, Ohio, Hall of Fame

Ohio Aviation Trades Association Sparky Award

Ohio Governor's Award

Ohio Women's Hall of Fame

Phi Mu Chapter of Spokane, Washington, Special Award

Special Award of Bexley Civic Association

Sports Woman of the Year, *Columbus Citizen-Journal*

Women in Aviation Pioneer Hall of Fame

Women's Aero Association of Wichita Award

The United States Air Force named a street (Jerrie Mock Avenue) in honor of Mock at Rickenbacker AFB (presently Rickenbacker Air National Guard Base and Rickenbacker International Airport) in Lockbourne, Ohio, located near Columbus.

Keys to the Cities

Bexley, Ohio

Burlington, North Carolina

Cincinnati, Ohio

Erie, Pennsylvania

Las Vegas, Nevada

St. Louis, Missouri

Toledo, Ohio

Wichita Falls, Texas

Wichita, Kansas

Xenia, Ohio

Glossary

ADF (automatic direction finder): a radio compass used for long-range navigation, which receives both a ground-station-identification signal and a direction signal that cause the needle to point toward that ground station

afterburners: a device used to increase the thrust of an engine by burning additional fuel in the hot exhaust gases

altitude: the height of a thing above a reference point, such as sea level or the earth's surface

autopilot: a computerized system that flies an airplane automatically on a preset course and at a preset altitude without the pilot handling the controls

aviatrix (pl. aviatrices): a woman pilot

Buckeye State: a nickname for the state of Ohio

cablegram: a message transmitted by telegraph

caviar: the roe (eggs) of a large fish, often eaten as a delicacy

checklist: a list of things or tasks to be checked off as each one is completed

circumnavigate: to sail or fly completely around something

clearance: the permission for a vehicle or an aircraft to proceed

closed course: a circuit that starts and finishes in the same spot

cockpit: the space within an airplane set apart for the pilot and/or copilot to sit and fly the plane

component: a part or element of a larger whole, especially a part of a machine or vehicle

Consolan (consolidated [low- or medium-frequency] long-range aid to navigation): a long-range navigational system designed basically for ships, but which can be used by aircraft through the ADF

consulate: a government office established in a foreign country to represent the interests of that government and its citizens there

cowl (or cowling): a removable metal covering over an aircraft engine

customs: a government department or agency that collects the taxes on imported goods and checks the legal papers of visitors from other countries

dead reckoning: a calculation to determine position using course, speed, time, and distance to be traveled

dialect: a variation of a language whose pronunciation, grammar, or vocabulary may differ from that of the standard language of the culture

foggles: goggles worn by a pilot during instrument flight training, which blind the pilot to everything but the instrument panel

gale-force winds: a wind having a speed of approximately thirty-two to sixty-three miles per hour

IFR (instrument flight rules): regulations under which flights are conducted when visibility is poor

low ceiling: a layer of low clouds

knot: a unit of speed for one nautical mile per hour (or 1.15 miles per hour)

magneto: a self-contained ignition system that uses magnets to create a spark to burn fuel

nautical mile: a unit of length used in sea and air navigation, based on the length of one minute of arc of a great circle, especially an international and U.S. unit equal to 6,076 feet

navigator: a device or person that calculates and directs a course

navigation maps: maps drawn up to plan a route or direction of travel

rice paddy (pl. rice paddies): a small, level flooded field used to grow rice in southern and eastern Asia

rickshaw: a two-wheeled carriage pulled along by a person

sari: an outer garment of lightweight cloth with one end wrapped about the waist to form a skirt and the other draped over the shoulder or head

squall: a violent change in weather caused when cold air replaces warm air

statute mile: a unit of length used for land travel, equal to 5,280 feet

strut: a bar or brace to support a structure from the side

sundial: a simple timekeeping device in which the shadow cast by a vertical pole is used to indicate the time of day

surveillance radar approach: an instrument-landing approach to a field following directions given by the tower controller who is watching the aircraft on a radar scope

tarmac: a term used to refer to paved areas at airports

throttle: a lever or pedal that regulates the fuel-air mixture and thus controls the speed of the engine

visual flight rules: fair conditions under which a pilot can navigate using landmarks, the ground, and the clouds

Acknowledgments

First, I'd like to thank the amazing Jerrie Mock for inviting me into her home and sharing her incredible story with me. I'd also like to thank my life-long friend, Carol Neale, for graciously offering to "ride alongside" me every step of the way as I wrote this book. You made the whole process fun—from sorting out photos, to reading first drafts, and taking the "road trip" with me to visit Jerrie. And thanks to Eddie Mock, Jerrie's grandson, who made Carol and me feel at home and helped us with a big smile and generous spirit. Richard Fauble, host of the McFarlin House, also made us feel at home away from home in Quincy, Florida.

Special thanks to my mom and former librarian, Fran Roe Bono, who sharpened up her computer skills and helped me with research. Thanks to my mother-in-law, Florence Pimm, for believing in me and encouraging me to chase after this project from the very beginning.

Joshua Alexander, thanks so much for meeting me at the airport, helping me navigate the world of aeronautics, sharing your love of flying, and for an-swering my many phone calls and texts. Thanks also to Ken Blalock for sharing your expertise in navigation and to Dale Ratcliff for your assistance in every-thing aviation and for sharing your love for the Lord.

Hugs sent to Susan Reid, Jerrie's younger sister, for spending countless hours showing photos and sharing family stories, and for graciously giving me a tour of your hometown of Newark, Ohio. Thanks for your friendship and for reading the first draft with the eyes of a teacher. Most of all, thanks for always believing in this book. Your enthusiasm was priceless!

A special thanks to Wendy Hollinger, Dale Ratcliff, and Judy Blair of Phoenix Graphix for formatting and donating all of their incredible photos and taking so much of their time and talents to make this book come alive. Wendy, Dale, and I want to shout Jerrie's story from the rooftops so more and more people will hear of the humble and brave Jerrie Mock and her historic feat of 1964.

I also want to give a big thank you to my wonderful critique group in central Ohio—Margaret Peterson-Haddix, Jenny Patton, Linda Stanek, Linda

Gerber, Amjed Qamar, and Erin MacLellan. I am blessed to be a part of such an amazing group. Thanks to Mary Biscuso and the helpful and friendly crew at the Dublin library, Cheryl Lubow from the State Library of Ohio, Nick Taggart from the Columbus Metropolitan Library, and Jennifer Lusetti from the Licking County Historical Society for all of your research assistance. Thanks to my early readers, Amy King, Lisa Koch, Shirley-Brooks Jones, Jill Nelson, Susan Reid, my sister Kathleen O'Connor, and Dr. Don Lewis for your helpful comments. Thanks to my friend and neighbor, Donna Miller Drake, for lending me your camera for the day. And thanks for the investigative work of Tanya Anderson, Eddie Mock, and Shirley Brooks-Jones.

I'd like to thank my family, especially my husband, Ed, for putting up with me as I became more and more obsessed with the story of Jerrie Mock. The more facts I uncovered, the more amazed and intrigued I became, and the more time I spent researching and writing. Even my grandsons Tommy and Sammy began to wonder if Jerrie Mock was a part of the family!

I am thankful for my editor, Michelle Houts, for always giving great advice and for working so hard, but most of all for her friendship. I am much obliged to Chiquita Babb for her enthusiasm and diligence in editing this story. And a great big thanks to Gillian Berchowitz, Ricky Huard, John and Beth Pratt, Samara Rafert, Jeff Kallet, Sally Welch, Maryann Gunderson, and the other folks at Ohio University Press for believing in me and for believing in Jerrie Mock.

Notes

Flight One

1. "Jerrie Mock makes last-minute preparations for her history-making, around-the-world solo flight which will begin 3/19," *Columbus Dispatch,* March 18, 1964, 1A.
2. Jerrie Mock, *Three-Eight Charlie* (Granville, OH: Phoenix Graphix Publishing Services, 2014), 2.
3. Ibid., 7.
4. "Jerrie Mock, 2490 Bexford Pl, Bexley, will take off March 18th in her attempt to set a women's around-the-world solo flight record," *Columbus Dispatch*, March 17, 1964, 3A.
5. Jerrie Mock, "My Flight through Fear," *GRIT,* Family Section, June 6, 1976, 14.
6. Ibid.
7. Richard Platt, *Experience Flight* (New York: Dorling Kindersley, 2006), 22.
8. Candace Fleming, *Amelia Lost: The Life and Disappearance of Amelia Earhart* (New York: Schwartz & Wade Books, 2011), 102.
9. Mock, *Three-Eight Charlie,* 10.
10. Jerrie Mock, interview by the author, Quincy, FL, July 30, 2014.

Flight Two

1. Jerrie Mock, interview by the author, Quincy, FL, July 30, 2014.
2. Jerrie Mock, telephone interview, June 5, 2014.
3. Ibid.
4. Ibid.
5. Mock, interview, July 30, 2014.
6. Susan Fredritz Reid (sister of Jerrie Mock), interview, January 20, 2015.
7. Jerrie Mock, interview by the author, Quincy, FL, July 31, 2014.

8. Amy Saunders, "How an Ohio Housewife Flew Around the World, Made History, and Was Then Forgotten," *Buzzfeed,* April 12, 2014.

9. Major Frank Chandler, "Base Man Was Navigator for Jerrie Mock's Flight," *Lockbourne Skyhawk,* May 15, 1964, 2.

10. "Jerrie Mock leaves Tripoli, Libya, and heads for Cairo, Egypt," *Columbus Evening Dispatch,* April 1, 1964, 1A.

Flight Three

1. Jerrie Mock, *Three-Eight Charlie* (Granville, OH: Phoenix Graphix Publishing Services, 2014), 14.

2. Ibid., 22.

3. Jerrie Mock, telephone interview, June 5, 2014.

Flight Four

1. "Mock is ready to take off for the Azores," *Columbus Dispatch,* March 26, 1964, 1A.

2. Jerrie Mock, *Three-Eight Charlie* (Granville, OH: Phoenix Graphix Publishing Services, 2014), 37.

3. Ibid., 41.

Flight Five

1. "Jerrie Mock flies into aviation history books when she completes a flight from the US to Africa; no other woman has ever piloted an airplane over this route," *Columbus Sunday Dispatch,* March 29, 1964, 1A.

2. Jerrie Mock, *Three-Eight Charlie* (Granville, OH: Phoenix Graphix Publishing Services, 2014), 45.

3. Ibid.

4. Jerrie Mock, interview by the author, Quincy, FL, July 31, 2014.

5. "Jerrie Mock flies into aviation history books," *Columbus Sunday Dispatch.*

6. "Jerrie Mock takes off in good weather for Bône, an Algerian city on the Mediterranean Sea, 910 miles farther along on her planned around-the-world flight route," *Columbus Dispatch,* March 30, 1964, 1A.

7. Mock, interview, July 31, 2014.

8. Mock, *Three-Eight Charlie*, 58.

9. "Jerrie Mock takes off in good weather for Bône," *Columbus Dispatch.*

Flight Six

1. Jerrie Mock, *Three-Eight Charlie* (Granville, OH: Phoenix Graphix Publishing Services, 2014), 64.

2. Ibid., 67.

3. Jerrie Mock, interview by the author, Quincy, FL, July 30, 2014.

4. Mock, *Three-Eight Charlie*, 60.

5. Ibid., 76.

6. Jerrie Mock, "My Flight through Fear," *GRIT,* Family Section, June 6, 1976, 14.

7. Mock, *Three-Eight Charlie*, 83.

8. Kathy Wesley, "Aviator from Newark broke world record," *Newark (OH) Advocate,* November 4, 1991.

Flight Seven

1. Jerrie Mock, *Three-Eight Charlie* (Granville, OH: Phoenix Graphix Publishing Services, 2014), 97.

2. Ibid., 100.

3. "Jerrie Mock takes off from the Cairo airport and heads for Dhahran, Saudi Arabia," *Columbus Dispatch,* April 3, 1964, 1A.

4. Mock, *Three-Eight Charlie*, 115.

5. Ibid., 123.

Flight Eight

1. Jerrie Mock, *Three-Eight Charlie* (Granville, OH: Phoenix Graphix Publishing Services, 2014), 128.

2. Ibid., 138.

3. Ibid., 140.

4. Ibid., 141.

Flight Nine

1. Jerrie Mock, *Three-Eight Charlie* (Granville, OH: Phoenix Graphix Publishing Services, 2014), 150.

2. Jerrie Mock, interview by the author, Quincy, FL, July 30, 2014.

3. Mock, *Three-Eight Charlie*, 170.

4. Ibid., 180.

5. Ibid., 192.

Flight Ten

1. Jerrie Mock, *Three-Eight Charlie* (Granville, OH: Phoenix Graphix Publishing Services, 2014), 186.

2. Angel Sablan, "The History Behind the Holiday," *Explore Guam. A monthly publication of the Pacific Daily News*, http://www.archive.guampdn.com/guampublishing/special-sections/exploreguam/pg5.html.

3. "Jerrie Mock recounts her thrilling global flight," *Columbus Sunday Dispatch*, April 19, 1964, 1A.

4. Mock, *Three-Eight Charlie*, 197.

5. Ibid., 198.

6. Ibid., 213.

7. Curby Rule, "The Deeper Meaning of Aloha," Aloha International, http://www.huna.org/html/deeper.html.

8. Mock, *Three-Eight Charlie*, 216.

Flight Eleven

1. Jerrie Mock, *Three-Eight Charlie* (Granville, OH: Phoenix Graphix Publishing Services, 2014), 232.

2. Ibid., 234.

3. Ibid., 241.

4. Ibid., 243.

5. Betty Vail and Edwards Dixon, "Winner Takes All," *Flying*, July 1964, 66.

6. Mock, *Three-Eight Charlie*, 247.

7. "Jerrie Mock recounts her thrilling global flight," *Columbus Sunday Dispatch*, April 19, 1964, 1A.

8. Mock, *Three-Eight Charlie*, 233.

Flight Twelve

1. Betty Vail and Edwards Dixon, "Winner Takes All," *Flying,* July 1964, 66.

2. Ibid.

3. Carolyn Focht, "Jerrie Mock wants to settle back into her normal routine, but her new celebrity status makes it rather difficult," *Columbus Sunday Dispatch,* April 19, 1964, 1A.

4. Vail and Dixon, "Winner Takes All."

5. Jerrie Mock, telephone interview, June 26, 2014.

6. James Craig, "Jet fighter ride thrills Jerrie Mock," *Columbus Dispatch,* July 15, 1964, 1B.

7. Jerrie Mock, interview by the author, Quincy, FL, July 31, 2014.

8. Captain Nancy W. Aldrich, "Marina Raskova," *20th Century Aviation Magazine,* 20thcenturyaviationmagazine.com/0-capt-nancy-aldrich/marina -raskova/.

9. "Jerrie Mock recounts her thrilling global flight," *Columbus Sunday Dispatch,* April 19, 1964, 1A.

10. Mock, telephone interview, June 26, 2014.

11. Timothy R. Gaffney, "Flying housewife scores multiple firsts," Century of Flight, Great Moments in Aviation, *Dayton (OH) Daily News,* April 15, 2002, 1B, http://nl.newsbank.com/nl-search/we/Archives?p_action=doc&p_docid= 0F3A4CCDF77794E8&p_docnum=1.

12. Mock, interview, July 31, 2014.

13. Lois Becker, "Globetrotter: Jerrie Mock and her trusty plane Charlie made aviation history," *Ohio State Alumni Magazine,* July–August 2014, 28–30.

14. "Jerrie Mock recounts her thrilling global flight," *Columbus Sunday Dispatch,* April 19, 1964, 1A.

Bibliography

Books

Fleming, Candace. *Amelia Lost: The Life and Disappearance of Amelia Earhart.* New York: Schwartz & Wade Books, 2011.

Haulman, Daniel L. *One Hundred Years of Flight: USAF Chronology of Significant Air and Space Events, 1903–2002.* Maxwell AFB, AL: Air Force History and Museums Program in association with Air University Press, 2003.

Johnson, Bobby H., and Stanley R. Mohler. *Wiley Post, His Winnie Mae, and the World's First Pressure Suit.* Washington, D.C.: Smithsonian Institution Press, 1971.

Mock, Jerrie. *Three-Eight Charlie.* Granville, OH: Phoenix Graphix Publishing Services, 2014.

Platt, Richard. *Experience Flight.* New York: Dorling Kindersley, 2006.

Web Sources

Cochrane, D. "Geraldine Mock." Women in Aviation and Space History. Smithsonian National Air and Space Museum. https://airandspace.si.edu/explore-and-learn/topics/women-in-aviation/mock.cfm.

Flank, Lenny. "The 'Spirit of Columbus': The First Woman to Fly Around the World." Hidden History, September 26, 2014. https://lflank.wordpress.com/2014/09/26/the-spirit-of-columbus-the-first-woman-to-fly-around-the-world/.

HistoryNet. "Jerrie Mock: Record-Breaking American Female Pilot." June 12, 2006. http://www.historynet.com/jerrie-mock-record-breaking-american-female-pilot.htm.

Meunier, Claude. Solo Flights Around the World, 2007. http://www.soloflights.org/index.html.

MyFlightBlog.com. "Missed by History: Jerrie Mock The First Woman to Fly Around the World," March 13, 2014. http://www.myflightblog.com/archives/missed-by-history-jerrie-mock-the-first-woman-to-fly-ar.php.

Saunders, Amy. "How an Ohio Housewife Flew Around the World, Made History, and Was Then Forgotten." *Buzzfeed,* April 12, 2014.

Saunders, Amy. "Where Amelia Tried, Geraldine Mock Succeeded." *Air & Space Magazine,* Smithsonian Institute, May 2014. http://www.airspacemag .com/history-of-flight/twenty-seven-years-after-amelia-earhart-tried -geraldine-mock-flew-solo-around-world-180950144/?no-ist.

Interviews

Jerrie Mock telephone interviews. June 5, June 26, July 8, and July 23, 2014.

Jerrie Mock personal interviews, Quincy, FL. July 30, July 31, and August 1, 2014.

Susan Fredritz Reid (Jerrie Mock's sister) personal interviews. August 26, 2014, and January 10, 2015.

Magazines

Aldrich, Captain Nancy W. "Marina Raskova." *20th Century Aviation Magazine.* 20thcenturyaviationmagazine.com/o-capt-nancy-aldrich/marina-raskova/.

Becker, Lois. "Globetrotter: Jerrie Mock and her trusty plane Charlie made aviation history." *Ohio State Alumni Magazine,* July–August 2014.

Fisher, Herb. Champion Spark Plug advertisement. *Flying,* August 1964.

Sablan, Angel. "The History Behind the Holiday." *Explore Guam. A monthly publication of the Pacific Daily News.* http://www.archive.guampdn.com/ guampublishing/special-sections/exploreguam/pg5.html.

Sunny 95. "2014 20 Outstanding Women." http://sunny95.com/outstanding -women/2014-20-outstanding-women-honorees/.

Vail, Betty, and Dixon Edwards. "Winner Takes All." *Flying,* July 1964.

Newspapers

Columbus (OH) Dispatch. March 17, 18, 26, 29, 30, 1964. April 1, 3, 19, 1964. July 15, 1964.

Dayton (OH) Daily News. April 15, 2002.

Newark (OH) Advocate. November 4, 1991.

BIOGRAPHIES FOR YOUNG READERS

Michelle Houts, Series Editor